T. Lobsang Rampa

Doctor
From Lhasa

CORGI BOOKS
TRANSWORLD PUBLISHERS LTD
A National General Company

DOCTOR FROM LHASA

A CORGI BOOK 0 552 07146 3

Originally published in Great Britain
by Souvenir Press Limited

PRINTING HISTORY
Souvenir Press Edition published 1959
Fourth Impression 1960
Corgi Edition published 1960
Corgi Edition reprinted 1963
Corgi Edition reissued 1965
Corgi Edition reprinted 1966
Corgi Edition reprinted 1968
Corgi Edition reprinted 1968
Corgi Edition reprinted 1970
Corgi Edition reprinted 1971

© 1959 C. Kuon Suo

This book is set in 10/12 pt. Times

Corgi Books are published by Transworld Publishers Ltd.,
Cavendish House, 57–59 Uxbridge Road,
Ealing, London, W.5.
Made and printed in Great Britain by
Hunt Barnard Printing Ltd., Aylesbury, Bucks.

CONTENTS

	Publishers' Note	6
	Author's Foreword	7
1	Into the Unknown	15
2	Chungking	32
3	Medical Days	52
4	Flying	69
5	The Other Side of Death	95
6	Clairvoyance	117
7	Mercy Flight	132
8	When the World was Very Young	151
9	Prisoner of the Japanese	172
10	How to Breathe	189
11	The Bomb	209

PUBLISHERS' NOTE

When Lobsang Rampa's first book *The Third Eye* was published, a very heated controversy arose which is still continuing. The contention of the author that a Tibetan lama was writing of his life "through" him, and had in fact fully occupied his body following a slight concussive accident, was not one to which many readers in the West were likely to give credence. Some, remembering similar cases in the past, although not from Tibet, preferred to keep an open mind. Others, and it is likely that they formed the majority, were openly sceptical. Many of them, however, whether they were specialists on the Far East or ordinary readers who enjoy an unusual book, were confounded by the author's obvious mastery of his subject, opening wide a door on a fascinating and little-known part of the world, and by the absence of any record of previous literary ability. Certainly no one was able to disprove his facts.

The present Publishers believe that, whatever the truth of the matter should be (if it is ever ascertainable), it is right that *The Third Eye* and now *Doctor from Lhasa* should be available to the public, if only because they are highly enjoyable books on their own merit. On the larger, fundamental issues which they raise, every reader must come to a personal decision. *Doctor from Lhasa* is as Lobsang Rampa wrote it. It must speak for itself.

Author's Foreword

WHEN I was in England I wrote *The Third Eye*, a book which is true, but which has caused much comment. Letters came in from all over the world, and in answer to requests I wrote this book, *Doctor from Lhasa*.

My experiences, as will be told in a third book, have been far beyond that which most people have to endure, experiences which are paralleled only in a few cases in history. That, though, is not the object of *this* book which deals with a continuation of my autobiography.

I am a Tibetan lama who came to the western world in pursuance of his destiny, came as was foretold, and endured all the hardships as foretold. Unfortunately, western people looked upon me as a curio, as a specimen who should be put in a cage and shown off as a freak from the unknown. It made me wonder what would happen to my old friends, the Yetis, if the westerners got hold of them— as they are trying to do.

Undoubtedly the Yeti would be shot, stuffed, and put in some museum. Even then people would argue and say that there were no such things as Yetis! To me it is strange beyond belief that western people can believe in television, and in space rockets that may circle the Moon and return and yet not credit Yetis or "Unknown Flying Objects," or, in fact, anything which they cannot hold in their hands and pull to pieces to see what makes it work.

But now I have the formidable task of putting into just a few pages that which before took a whole book, the details of my early childhood. I came of a very high-ranking family, one of the leading families in Lhasa, the capital of

7

Tibet. My parents had much to say in the control of the country, and because I was of high rank I was given severe training so that, it was considered, I should be fit to take my place. Then, before I was seven years of age, in accordance with our established custom, the Astrologer Priests of Tibet were consulted to see what type of career would be open to me. For days before this preparations went forward, preparations for an immense party at which all the leading citizens, all the notabilities of Lhasa would come to hear my fate. Eventually the Day of Prophecy arrived. Our estate was thronged with people. The Astrologers came armed with their sheets of paper, with their charts, and with all the essentials of their profession. Then, at the appropriate time, when everyone had been built up to a high pitch of excitement, the Chief Astrologer pronounced his findings. It was solemnly proclaimed that I should enter a lamasery at the age of seven, and be trained as a priest, and as a priest surgeon. Many predictions were made about my life, in fact the whole of my life was outlined. To my great sorrow everything they said has come true. I say "sorrow" because most of it has been misfortune, and hardship, and suffering, and it does not make it any easier when one knows all that one is to suffer.

I entered the Chakpori lamasery when I was seven years of age, making my lonely way along the path. At the entrance I was kept, and had to undergo an ordeal to see if I was hard enough, tough enough to undergo the training. This I passed, and then I was allowed to enter. I went through all the stages from an absolutely raw beginner, and in the end I became a lama, and an abbot. Medicine and surgery were my particular strong points. I studied these with avidity, and I was given every facility to study dead bodies. It is a belief in the west that the lamas of Tibet never do anything to bodies if it means making an opening. The belief is, apparently, that Tibetan medical science is rudimentary, because the medical lamas treat only the

8

exterior and not the interior. That is not correct. The ordinary lama, I agree, never opens a body, it is against his own form of belief. But there was a special nucleus of lamas, of whom I was one, who were trained to do operations, and to do operations which were possibly even beyond the scope of western science.

In passing there is also a belief in the west that Tibetan medicine teaches that the man has his heart on one side, and the woman has her heart on the other side. Nothing could be more ridiculous. Information such as this has been passed on to the western people by those who have no real knowledge of what they are writing about, because some of the charts to which they refer deal with astral bodies instead, a very different matter. However, that has nothing to do with this book.

My training was very intensive indeed, because I had to know not only my specialised subjects of medicine and surgery, but all the Scriptures as well because, as well as being a medical lama, I also had to pass as a religious one, as a fully trained priest. So it was necessary to study for two branches at once, and that meant studying twice as hard as the average. I did not look upon that with any great favour!

But it was not all hardship, of course. I took many trips to the higher parts of Tibet—Lhasa is 12,000 feet above sea level—gathering herbs, because we based our medical training upon herbal treatment, and at Chakpori we always had at least 6,000 different types of herb in stock. We Tibetans believe that we know more about herbal treatment than people in any other part of the world. Now that I have been around the world several times that belief is strengthened.

On several of my trips to the higher parts of Tibet I flew in man-lifting kites, soaring above the jagged peaks of the high mountain ranges, and looking for miles, and miles, over the countryside. I also took part in a memorable

9

expedition to the almost inaccessible part of Tibet, to the highest part of the Chang Tang Highlands. Here, we of the expedition found a deeply secluded valley between clefts in the rock, and warmed, warmed by the eternal fires of the earth, which caused hot waters to bubble out and flow into the river. We found, too, a mighty city, half of it exposed in the hot air of the hidden valley, and the other half buried in the clear ice of a glacier. Ice so clear that the other part of the city was visible as if through the very clearest water. That part of the city which has been thawed out was almost intact. The years had dealt gently indeed with the buildings. The still air, the absence of wind, had saved the buildings from damage by attrition. We walked along the streets, the first people to tread those streets for thousands and thousands of years. We wandered at will through houses which looked as if they were awaiting their owners, until we looked a little more closely and saw strange skeletons, petrified skeletons, and then we realised that here was a dead city. There were many fantastic devices which indicated that this hidden valley had once been the home of a civilisation far greater than any now upon the face of the earth. It proved conclusively to us that we were now as savages compared to the people of that bygone age. But in this, the second book, I write more of that city.

When I was quite young I had a special operation which was called the opening of the third eye. In it a sliver of hard wood, which had been soaked in special herbal solutions, was inserted in the centre of my forehead in order to stimulate a gland which gave me increased powers of clairvoyance. I was born markedly clairvoyant, but then, after the operation, I was really abnormally so, and I could see people with their aura around them as if they were wreathed in flames of fluctuating colours. From their auras I could divine their thoughts; what ailed them, what their hopes and fears were. Now that I have left Tibet I am trying to interest western doctors in a device which would enable

10

any doctor and surgeon to see if the human aura as it really is, in colour. I know that if doctors and surgeons can see the aura, they can see what really affects a person. So that by looking at the colours, and by the outline of the moving bands, the specialist can tell exactly what illnesses a person is suffering from. Moreover, this can be told before there is any visible sign in the physical body itself, because the aura shows evidence of cancer, TB, and other complaints, many months before it attacks the physical body. Thus, by having such early warning of the onset of disease the doctor can treat the complaint, and cure it infallibly. To my horror, and very deep sorrow, western doctors are not at all interested. They appear to think it is something to do with magic, instead of being just ordinary common sense, as it is. Any engineer will know that high tension wires have a corona around them. So has the human body, and it is just an ordinary physical thing which I want to show to the specialists, and they reject it. That is a tragedy. But it will come in time. The tragedy is that so many people must suffer and die needlessly, until it does come.

The Dalai Lama, the thirteenth Dalai Lama, was my patron. He ordered that I should receive every possible assistance in training, and in experience. He directed that I should be taught everything that could be crammed into me, and as well as being taught by the ordinary oral system I was also instructed by hypnosis, and by various other forms which there is no need to mention here. Some of them are dealt with in this book, or in *The Third Eye*. Others are so novel, and so incredible that the time is not ripe for them to be discussed.

Because of my powers of clairvoyance I was able to be of a great assistance to the Inmost One on various occasions. I was hidden in his audience room so that I could interpret a person's real thoughts and intentions from the aura. This was done to see if the person's speech and thoughts tallied particularly when they were foreign statesmen visiting the

11

Dalai Lama. I was an unseen observer when a Chinese delegation was received by the Great Thirteenth. I was an unseen observer, too, when an Englishman went to see the Dalai Lama, but on the latter occasion I nearly fell down in my duty because of my astonishment at the remarkable dress which the man wore, my first, very first sight of European dress!

The training was long and arduous. There were temple services to be attended throughout the night as well as throughout the day. Not for us the softness of beds. We rolled ourself in our solitary blanket, and went to sleep on the floor. The teachers were strict indeed, and we had to study, and learn, and commit everything to memory. We did not keep notebooks, we committed everything to memory. I learned metaphysical subjects as well. I went deeply into it, clairvoyance, astral travelling, telepathy, I went through the whole lot. In one of my stages of initiation I visited the secret caverns and tunnels beneath the Potala, caverns and tunnels of which the average man knows nothing. They are the relics of an age-old civilisation which is almost beyond memory, beyond racial memory almost, and on the walls were the records, pictorial records of things that flow in the air, and things that went beneath the earth. In another stage on initiation I saw the carefully preserved bodies of giants, ten feet, and fifteen feet long. I, too, was sent to the other side of death, to know that there is no death, and when I returned I was a Recognised Incarnation, with a rank of an abbot. But I did not want to be an abbot, tied to a lamasery. I wanted to be a lama, free to move about, free to help others, as the Prediction said I would. So, I was confirmed in the rank of lama by the Dalai Lama himself, and by Him I was attached to the Potala in Lhasa. Even then my training continued, I was taught various forms of western science, optics, and other allied subjects. But, at last the time came when I was called once again to the Dalai Lama, and given instructions.

He told me that I had learned all that I could learn in Tibet, that the time had come for me to move on, to leave all that I loved, all that I cared for. He told me that special messengers had been sent out to Chungking to enrol me as a student of medicine and surgery in that Chinese city.

I was sick at heart when I left the presence of the Inmost one, and made my way to my Guide, the lama Mingyar Dondup, and told him what had been decided. Then I went to the home of my parents to tell them also what had happened, that I was to leave Lhasa. The days flew by, and the final day came when I left Chakpori, when for the last time I saw Mingyar Dondup in the flesh, and I made my way out of the city of Lhasa, the Holy City, on to the high mountain passes. And as I looked back the last thing I saw was a symbol. For from the golden roofs of the Potala a solitary kite was flying.

CHAPTER ONE

Into the Unknown

NEVER before had I felt so cold, so hopeless, and so miserable. Even in the desolate wastes of the Chang Tang Highlands, 20,000 feet or more above sea level, where the grit-laden, sub-zero winds whipped and cut to blood-stained tatters any exposed skin, I had been warmer than now; there the cold was not so bitter as the fearsome chill I felt at my heart. I was leaving my beloved Lhasa. As I turned and saw behind me diminutive figures on the golden roofs of the Potala, and above them a solitary kite dipped and bobbed in the slight breeze, dipped and bobbed as if to say, "Farewell, your days of kite flying are over now, on to more serious matters." To me that kite was a symbol, a kite up in the immensity of blue, held to its home by a thin cord. I was going off to the immensity of the world beyond Tibet, held by the thin cord of my love for Lhasa. I was going to the strange, terrible world beyond my peaceful land. I was indeed sick at heart as I turned my back upon my home and with my fellows rode off into that great unknown. They too were unhappy, but they had the consolation of knowing that after leaving me at Chungking, 1,000 miles away, they could start off home. They would return, and on their journey back they would have the great consolation of knowing that every step they took brought them nearer to home. I had to continue ever on to strange lands, to strange people, and to stranger and stranger experiences.

The prophecy made about my future when I was seven years old had said that I should enter a lamasery and be trained first as a chela, then on to the state of a trappa, and so on, until in the fulness of time I could pass the examination of a lama. From that point, so the astrologers said, I was to leave Tibet, leave my home, leave all that I loved, and go out into what we termed barbarian China. I would journey to Chungking and study to become a doctor and surgeon. According to the Priest Astrologers I would be involved in wars, I would be a prisoner of strange peoples, and I would have to rise above all temptation, all suffering, to bring help to those in need. They told me that my life would be hard, that suffering and pain and ingratitude would be my constant companions. How right they were!

So with these thoughts in my mind—not by any means cheerful thoughts—I gave the order to carry on forward. As a precaution when we were just beyond sight of Lhasa we dismounted from our horses and made sure that they were comfortable, that the saddles were not too tight, nor yet too loose. Our horses were to be our constant friends on the journey, and we had to look after them at least as well as we looked after ourselves. With that settled and with the consolation of knowing that our horses were at ease, we remounted and resolutely set our gaze forward, and rode on.

It was early in 1927 when we left Lhasa and made our slow, slow way to Chotang on the river Brahmaputra. We had had many discussions as to the most suitable route, and this, by way of the river and Kanting, was recommended as being the most suitable. The Brahmaputra is a river which I know well, having flown above one of its sources in a range on the Himalayas when I had been fortunate enough to fly a man-lifting kite. We, in Tibet, regarded the river with reverence, but nothing like the reverence with which it was regarded elsewhere. Hundreds of miles away where it rushed down to the Bay of Bengal, it was deemed to be sacred, almost as sacred as Benares. It was the Brahmaputra, so we were told, which made the Bay of Bengal. In the early days of history the river was

16

swift, and deep too, and as it rushed down almost in a straight line from the mountains it scoured away at the soft soil and made the wonderful bay, the glorious bay. We followed the river through the mountain passes into Sikang. In the old days, the happy days, when I was very young, Sikang was part of Tibet, a province of Tibet. Then the British made an incursion into Lhasa. After that the Chinese were encouraged to invade and so they captured Sikang. With murderous intent they walked into that part of our country, killing, raping, and pillaging, and they took Sikang to themselves. They staffed it with Chinese officials, officials who had lost favour elsewhere were sent to Sikang as a form of punishment. Unfortunately for them the Chinese government gave them no support. They had to manage the best way they could. We found that these Chinese officials were mere puppets, helpless men, ineffectual, men at whom Tibetans laughed. Of course, at times we pretended to obey the Chinese officials, but that was mere politeness. When their back was turned we went our own way.

Our journey continued day after day. We made our halts convenient to bring us to a lamasery where we could stay the night. As I was a lama, indeed an abbot, a Recognised Incarnation, we were given the very best welcome which the monks could manage. Furthermore I was travelling under the personal protection of the Dalai Lama, and that indeed counted heavily.

We made our way to Kanting. This is a very famous market town, well known for its sale of yaks, but particularly famous as an exporting centre for the brick-tea which we found so palatable in Tibet. This tea was brought from China, it was not just ordinary tea leaves but more or less a chemical concoction. It had tea, bits of twig, soda, saltpetre, and a few other things in it because in Tibet food was not the plentiful commodity that it is in some other parts of the world, and our tea had to act as a form of soup as well

17

as drink. In Kanting the tea is mixed and made into blocks or bricks as they are more commonly called. These bricks were such a size and weight that they could be loaded upon horses, and later upon the yaks which would carry them over the high mountain ranges to Lhasa where they would be sold in the market and transported throughout Tibet.

Tea bricks had to be of special size and shape, but they also had to be specially packed so that if a horse stumbled in a mountain ford and tipped the tea into a river no harm would be done. These bricks were packed tightly into a green hide, or, as it is sometimes called, a raw hide, and were then quickly dipped in water. After this they would be put on rocks in the sun to dry. As they dried they shrank, they shrank amazingly, and they absolutely compressed the contents. In drying they took on a brown appearance and they were as hard as bakelite but very much stronger. Any of these hides when dried could be rolled down a mountainside and land safely and unharmed. It could be tipped into a river, and perhaps stay there a couple of days. When fished out and dried everything would be intact, no water would have entered so nothing would be spoilt. Our bricks of tea in their dried hide cases were among the most hygienic packages in the world. Tea, by the way, was often used as currency. A trader who had no money with him could break off a lump of tea and barter it. There was never any need to bother about cash while one had tea bricks.

Kanting impressed us with its businesslike turmoil. We were used only to our own Lhasa, but here in Kanting there were peoples from a lot of countries, from as far away as Japan, from India, Burma, and the nomad people from beyond the Takla mountains. We wandered in the market place, mixed with the traders and heard the strange voices and the different languages. We rubbed shoulders with monks of the different religions, of the Zen sect, and others. And then, marvelling at the novelty of it all, we made our way to a small lamasery on the road beyond Kanting. Here we were expected. In fact, our hosts were getting rather worried that we had not arrived. We soon told them that we had been looking in the market place, and listening to the market gossip. The abbot in charge made us very welcome and listened with avidity to our tales of Tibet, listened to the news we gave, for we came from the seat of learning, the Potala, and we were the men who had been in the Chang Tang Highlands and seen great marvels. Our fame had indeed preceded us.

Early in the morning after we had attended the service in the temple we took to the road again on our horses, carrying a small amount of food, tsampa, with us. The road was a mere earth track high up on the sides of a gorge. Down below there were trees, more trees than any of us had ever seen before. Some were partly hidden by the mist set up by the spray of a waterfall. Giant rhododendrons also covered the gorge while the ground itself was carpeted with varied-hued flowers, small mountain flowers which scented the air and added colour to the scene. We, though, were oppressed and miserable, miserable at the thought of leaving home and oppressed by the density of the air. All the time we were getting lower and lower, and we were finding it more and more difficult to breathe. There was another difficulty with which we were afflicted; in Tibet where the air is thin water boils at a lower temperature and in the higher places we could drink tea which was actually boiling. We kept our tea and water on the fire until all the bubbles gave warning that it was ready to drink. At first, in this lower land, we suffered greatly from scalded lips as we tried to gauge the temperature of the water. It was our habit to drink the tea straight from the fire. We had to do so in Tibet otherwise the bitter cold would rob our tea of all heat. At that time we had no knowledge that the denser air would affect the boiling point, nor did it occur to us that we could wait for the boiling water to cool with no danger of it freezing.

We were seriously upset by the difficulty in breathing, by

the weight of air pressing on our chests and on our lungs. At first we thought it was emotion at leaving our beloved Tibet, but later we found that we were being suffocated, drowned by air. Never before had any of us been below 1,000 feet. Lhasa itself is 12,000 feet high. Frequently we were living at even greater heights, as when we went to the Chang Tang Highlands where we were above 20,000 feet. We had heard many tales in the past about Tibetans who had left Lhasa to go and seek their fortunes in the lowlands. Rumour said that they had died after months of misery with shattered lungs. The old wives' tales of the Holy City had definitely made much ado of the statement that those who left Lhasa to go to the lower lands went to their painful deaths. I knew that there was no truth in that because my own parents had been to Shanghai where they had much property, they had been there and had returned safely. I had had little to do with my parents because they were such busy people and in such a high position that they had no time for us children. My information had been gleaned from servants. But now I was seriously perturbed about the feelings we were experiencing; our lungs felt scorched, we felt that we had iron bands about our chests keeping us from breathing. Each breath was a shuddering effort, and if we moved too quickly pains, like pains of fire, shot through us. As we journeyed on, getting lower and lower, the air became thicker and the temperature warmer. It was a terrible climate for us. In Lhasa, in Tibet, the weather had been very cold indeed, but a dry cold, a healthy cold, and in conditions like that temperature mattered little, but now, in this thick air with so much moisture, we were almost at our wits' end to keep going. At one time the others tried to persuade me to order an about-turn, a return to Lhasa, saying that we would all die if we persisted in our foolhardy venture, but I, mindful of the prophecy, would have none of it. And so we journeyed on. As the temperature became warmer we became dizzy, intoxicated almost, and we seemed to have trouble with our eyes. We could not see as far as usual, nor so clearly, and our judgment of distances was all wrong. Much later I found the explanation. In Tibet there is the purest and cleanest air in the world, one can see for fifty miles or more, and as clearly as if it were but ten. Here, in the dense air of the low-lands, we could not see so far, and what we could see was distorted by the very thickness of the air and its impurities.

For many days we journeyed along, getting lower and lower, travelling through forests containing more trees than any of us had ever dreamed existed. There is not much wood in Tibet, not many trees, and for a time we could not resist getting off our horses and running to the different sorts of trees, touching them, smelling them. They were all so strange to us and in such plentitude. The rhododendrons of course were familiar because we had many rhododendrons in Tibet. Rhododendron blossom was, in fact, a luxury article of food when properly prepared. We rode on, marvelling at all we saw, marvelling at the difference between this and our home. I cannot say how long we took, how many days or how many hours, because such things did not interest us at all. We had plenty of time, we knew nothing of the scurry and bustle of civilization, nor if we had known would we have cared.

We rode about eight or ten hours a day and we stayed our nights at convenient lamaseries. They were not all of our own form of Buddhism, but no matter, we were always wel-come. With us, with the real Buddhists of the East, there is no rivalry, no friction or rancour, and a traveller was always welcome. As was our custom we took part in all the services while we were there. We lost no opportunity of conversing with the monks who were so keen to welcome us. Many were the strange tales they told us about the changing con-ditions in China; about how the old order of peace was changing, how the Russians, "the men of the bear," were trying to indoctrinate the Chinese with political ideals, which to us, seemed completely wrong. It seemed to us that what the Russians were preaching was "What is yours, is mine; what is mine is staying mine!" The Japanese, as well, we were told, were making trouble in various parts of China. It appeared to be a question of over-population. Japan was producing too many children, and producing too little food, so—they were trying to invade peaceful peoples, trying to steal from them, as if only the Japanese mattered.

At last we left Sikang, and crossed the border into Szechwan. A few days more, and we came to the banks of the river Yangtze. Here, at a little village, we stopped late one afternoon. We stopped, not because we had got to our destination for the night, but because there was a milling throng ahead of us, a meeting of some sort. We edged our way forward, and, all of us being rather bulky, we had no difficulty at all in pushing our way to the front of the group. A tall white man was there, standing on an ox cart, gesticulating, telling of the wonders of Communism, trying to exhort the peasants to rise up and kill the landowners. He was waving about papers with pictures on, showing a sharp-featured, bearded man, calling him the Saviour of the world. But we were not impressed with the picture of Lenin, nor with the man's talk. We turned away in disgust, and carried on for a few miles more to the lamasery at which we were going to stay the night.

There were lamaseries in various parts of China as well as the Chinese monasteries and temples. For some people, particularly in Sikang, Szechwan, or Chinghai, prefer the form of Buddhism of Tibet, and so our lamaseries were there to teach those who were in need of our assistance. We never sought converts, we never asked people to join us, for we believed that all men were free to choose. We had no love of those missionaries who went about ranting that one had to join such and such a religion to be saved. We knew that when a person wanted to become a lamaist they would become so without any persuading on our part. We knew how we had laughed at missionaries who came to Tibet, who came to China; it was a standing joke that people would pretend to be converted just to get the gifts and the other, so-called, advantages which the missionaries were dispensing. And another thing, Tibetans and the old order of Chinese were polite folk, they tried to cheer the missionaries, tried to make them believe that they were having some success, but never for one moment did we believe what they were telling us. We knew that they had their belief, but we preferred to keep our own.

We travelled on and followed the course of the river Yangtse, the river which I was later to know so well, because this was a pleasanter path. We were fascinated in watching the vessels on the river. We had never seen boats before although some of us had seen pictures of them, and I had once seen a steam ship in a special clairvoyant session which I had had with my Guide, the Lama Mingyar Dondup. But that is detailed later in this book. In Tibet our boatmen used coracles. These were very light frames covered with yak-skin, and they would carry perhaps four or five passengers besides the boatman. Often an unpaying passenger would be the goat which was the boatman's pet, but which also did its share on land because the boatman would load his own personal belongings, his bundle or his blankets on to the goat's back while he would shoulder the coracle and climb the rocks to avoid the rapids which otherwise would wreck his boat. Sometimes a farmer who wanted to cross a river would use a goatskin or a yak-skin which had legs and other openings sealed off. He would use this contraption in much the same way as Westerners use water-wings. But now, we were interested to see real boats with sails, lateen sails, flapping in the wind.

One day we drew to a halt near some shallows. We were intrigued; two men were walking in the river with a long net between them. Ahead of them two more men were beating the water with sticks and yelling horribly. We thought at first that these were madmen, and the ones with the net

23

were following them to try to take them into custody. We watched, and then, at a signal from one of the men, the clamour stopped and the two with the net walked together so that their paths crossed. Between them they drew taut the two ends of the net, and dragged it ashore. Safely up on the sandy bank they tipped the net out and pounds and pounds of shining, struggling fish dropped to the ground. It shocked us because we never killed. We believed that it was very wrong to kill any living creature. In our own rivers in Tibet fish would come to touch a hand stretched in the water toward them. They would take food from one's hands. They had no fear whatever of man, and were often pets. But here, in China, they were just food. We wondered how these Chinese could claim to be Buddhists when they so blatantly killed for their own gain.

We had dallied too long; we had sat by the side of the river for an hour, perhaps two hours, and we were unable to reach a lamasery that night. We shrugged our shoulders in resignation and prepared to camp by the side of the path. A little to the left, however, was a secluded grove of trees with the river running through and we made our way there, and dismounted, tethering our horses so that they could feed on the quite—to us—luxuriant herbage. It was a simple matter to gather sticks and to light a fire, then we boiled our tea, and ate our tsampa. For a time we sat around the fire, talking of Tibet, talking of what we had seen on our journey, and of our thoughts for the future. One by one my companions yawned, turned away and rolled themselves into the blankets and fell asleep. At last, as the glowing embers turned to blackness, I too rolled in my blanket and lay down, but not to sleep. I thought of all the hardships I had undergone. I thought of leaving my home at the age of seven, of entering a lamasery, of the hardships, the severe training. I thought of my expeditions to the Highlands, and further North to the great Chang Tang Highlands. I thought also of the Inmost One, as we called the

Dalai Lama, and then inevitably of my beloved Guide, the Lama Mingyar Dondup. I felt sick with apprehension, heartbroken, and then it seemed as if the countryside was lit up as if by the noonday sun. I looked in amazement, and I saw my Guide standing before me. "Lobsang! Lobsang!" he exclaimed, "Why are you so downhearted? Have you forgotten? Iron ore may think itself senselessly tortured in the furnace, but as the tempered steel blade looks back it knows better. You have had a hard time, Lobsang, but it is all for a good purpose. This, as we have so often discussed, is merely a world of illusion, a world of dreams. You have many hardships yet to face, many hard tests, but you will triumph, you will overcome them, and in the end you will accomplish the task which you have set out to do." I rubbed my eyes, then it occurred to me, of course, the Lama Mingyar Dondup had come to me by astral travelling. I had often done things like that myself, but this was so unexpected, it showed me so plainly that he was thinking of me all the time, helping me with his thoughts.

For some time we communed with the past, dwelling upon my weaknesses, and feeling, with a transient warm glow of happiness, the many happy moments when we had been together, like father and son. He showed me, by mental pictures, some of the hardships to be encountered and—more happily—the eventual success which would come to me in spite of all attempts to prevent it. After an indeterminate time, the golden glow faded as my Guide reiterated his final words of hope and encouragement. With them as my predominant thoughts, I rolled over beneath the stars in the frozen night sky, and eventually fell asleep.

The next morning we were awake early and prepared our breakfast. As was our custom we held our morning service which I, as the senior ecclesiastical member, conducted, and then we continued our journey along the beaten earth track by the side of the river.

About midday the river bore away to the right and the

path went straight ahead; we followed it. It ended at what to us appeared to be a very wide road. Actually, as I know now, it was in fact a second class road, but we had never before seen a man-made road of this type. We rode along it, marvelling at the texture of it, marvelling at the comfort of not having to look out for roots to avoid, not having to look for pot-holes. We jogged along thinking that in two or three more days we would be at Chungking. Then, something about the atmosphere, something unexplained, made us glance at each other uneasily. One of us happened to look up to the far horizon. Then he stood upright in his stirrups in alarm, wide-eyed and gesticulating. "Look!" he said. "A dust storm is approaching." He pointed ahead to where there was most certainly a grey-black cloud approaching at considerable speed. In Tibet there are dust clouds; clouds of grit-laden air travelling at perhaps eighty miles an hour or more, from which all people except the yak must shelter. The yak's thick wool protects it from harm, but all other creatures, particularly humans, are lacerated and made to bleed by the stinging grit which scratches the face and hands. We were certainly disconcerted because this was the first dust storm we had seen since leaving Tibet, and we looked about us to see where we could shelter. But there did not appear to be anything suitable for us. To our consternation we became aware that the approaching cloud was accompanied by a most strange sound, a sound stranger than any of us had ever heard before; something like a temple trumpet being played by a tone-deaf learner, or, we thought miserably, like the legions of the devil marching upon us. Thrum-thrum-thrum, it went. Rapidly the roar increased and became stranger and stranger. There were clatters and rattles with it. We were almost too frightened to do anything, almost too frightened to think. The dust cloud sped toward us faster and faster. We were terrified and almost paralysed with fright. We thought again of the dust clouds in Tibet, but most certainly none had ever come at us with a roar. In panic we looked again to find some place of shelter, some place where we should be protected from this terrible storm which was coming upon us. Our horses were much quicker than we at making up their minds where to go; they broke formation, they reared and they bucked. I had an impression of flying hooves, and my horse gave a most ferocious whinny, and seemed to bend in the middle. There was a strange tug, and a feeling that something had broken. "Oh, my leg is torn off!" I thought. Then my horse and I parted company. I sailed through the air in an arc, and landed flat on my back at the side of the road, stunned. Rapidly the dust cloud came nearer, and I saw inside it the Devil himself, a roaring black monster, shaking and shuddering. It came and it passed. Flat on my back, head awhirl, I saw my first motor vehicle, a battered old ex-American lorry, travelling at its noisy top speed, driven by a grinning Chinese. The stench from it! Devil's breath, we called it later. A mixture of petrol, oil, and manure; the load of manure which it carried was gradually being bounced off, some of it was being jolted over the side to land with a splat beside me. With a clatter and a roar the lorry whizzed by, leaving clouds of choking dust, and a plume of black smoke from the exhaust. Soon it became a weaving dot in the distance, weaving from side to side of the road, the noise abated and there was no sound.

I looked about me in the silence. There was no sign of my companions; perhaps even worse, there was no sign of the horse! I was still trying to disentangle myself because the broken part of the girth had twisted round my legs, when the others appeared, one by one, looking shamefaced and highly nervous in case any other of these roaring demons should appear. We still did not quite know what we had seen. It was all too quick and the clouds of dust had obscured so much. The others sheepishly dismounted, and helped me to brush the dust of the road off my garments. At last I was presentable again but—where was that horse?

My companions had come from all directions, yet not one of them had seen my mount. We looked about, we called, we looked in the dust for any sign of hoof marks, but we could find no trace whatever. It seemed to us that the wretched animal must have jumped into the lorry and been carried off. No, we could find no trace whatever and we sat down by the side of the road to discuss what to do. One of my companions offered to stay at a nearby hut, so I could have his horse, and he would get back on his companions' return, when I should have been left at Chungking. But I would have none of this. I knew as well as he did that he wanted a rest and it did not solve the mystery of the missing horse.

My companions' horses whinnied and from a nearby Chinese peasant's hut a horse whinnied in reply. It was soon stifled as if by a hand over the nostrils. Light dawned upon us. We looked at each other and prepared for instant action. Now, why should a horse be inside that poverty-stricken hut? That ramshackle building was not the home of a man who would own a horse. Obviously the horse was being concealed from us. We jumped to our feet and looked about us for stout clubs. Finding no suitable weapons about we cut them from the nearby trees, and then we set off to the hut, a determined troup, suspicious of what was happening. The door was a rickety affair with thongs for hinges. Our polite knocking produced no reply. There was dead silence, not a sound. Our rude demands for entry elicited no response. Yet, previously a horse had whinnied and its whinny had been suppressed. So we made a fierce onslaught on that door. For a short time it withstood our efforts, then, as the thong hinges showed signs of parting and the door tilted and appeared to be on the point of collapse, it was hastily thrown open. Inside was a wizened Chinaman, his face contorted with terror. It was a wretched hovel, filthy, and the owner was a tattered rag-bag of a man. But that was not what interested us. Inside was my horse with a bag

28

round its muzzle to keep it quiet. We were not at all pleased with the Chinese peasant and indicated our disapproval in no uncertain manner. Under the pressure of our interrogation he admitted that he had tried to steal the horse from us. We, he said, were rich monks and could afford to lose a horse or two. He was just a poor peasant. By the look of him he thought we were going to kill him. We must have looked fierce. We had travelled perhaps eight hundred miles and we were tired and rough looking. However, we had no unpleasant designs upon him. Our combined knowledge of Chinese was entirely adequate to enable us to convey to him our opinion of his act, his probable end in this life, and his undoubted destination in the next. With that off our minds and most certainly on his, we resaddled the horse, being very careful that the girth band was secure, and again we set off for Chungking.

That night we stayed at a small lamasery, very small. It had six monks in it, but we were given every hospitality. The night after was the last night of our long journey. We came to a lamasery where, as the representatives of the Inmost One, we were greeted with that courtesy which we had come to consider as our due. Again we were given food and accommodation; we took part in their temple services, and talked far into the night about events in Tibet, about our journeys to the great Northern Highlands and about the Dalai Lama. I was very gratified to know that even here my Guide, the Lama Mingyar Dondup, was well known. I was interested too to meet a Japanese monk who had been to Lhasa and studied our form of Buddhism which is so different from that of the Zen.

There was much talk of impending changes in China, of revolution, of a new order, an order in which all the landowners were to be thrown out and illiterate peasants were to take their place. Russian agents were everywhere promising wonders, accomplishing nothing, nothing constructive. These Russians, to our mind, were agents of the

Devil, disrupting, corrupting, like plague destroying a body. The incense burned low and was replenished. It burned low again and again, and was replenished. We talked on; our talk was full of foreboding for the dire changes which were taking place. Men's values were distorted, matters of the soul were not considered to be valuable nowadays, but only transient power. The world was a very sick place. The stars rolled high in the sky. We talked on and at last one by one we lay down where we were to sleep. In the morning we knew our journey would come to an end. My journey for the time being, but my companions would return to Tibet leaving me alone in a strange unkind world where might was right. Sleep did not come to me easily that last night.

In the morning after the usual temple services and a very good meal we set out again on the road to Chungking, our horses much refreshed. Traffic was more numerous now. Lorries and various forms of wheeled vehicles abounded. Our horses were restive, frightened. They were not accustomed to the noise of all these vehicles and the smell of burnt petrol was a constant irritant to them. It was indeed an effort to stay in our high peaked saddles.

We were interested to see people working in the fields, the terraced fields, fertilized with human excreta. The people were clad in blue, the blue of China. They all seemed to be old, and they were very tired. They moved listlessly as if life was too great a burden for them or as if the spirit was crushed and there was nothing more worth living and striving for. Men, women and children worked together. We rode on, still following the course of the river which we had rejoined some miles back. At last we came in sight of the high cliffs on which the old city of Chungking was built. To us this was the very first sight of any city of note outside Tibet. We stopped and gazed in fascination, but my gaze held not a little dread of the new life which lay ahead before me.

In Tibet I had been a power in the land through my rank,

through my accomplishments and my close association with the Dalai Lama. Now, I had come to a foreign city as a student. It reminded me all too vividly of the hardships of my early days. So it was not with happiness that I gazed at the scene ahead. This, I well knew, was but a step on the long, long track, the track which would lead me to hardships, to strange countries, stranger even than China, to the West where men worshipped only gold.

Before us stretched rising ground with the terraced fields clinging precariously to the steep sides. At the top of the rise grew trees, which to us who had seen so few until recent days seemed to be a forest. Here, too, the blue-clad figures worked on in the distant fields, plodding along as their remote ancestors had plodded before them. One-wheeled carts drawn by small ponies rumbled along, laden with garden produce for the markets of Chungking. They were queer vehicles. The wheel came up through the centre of the cart, leaving space on each side for the goods. One such vehicle which we saw had an old woman balanced on one side of the wheel and two small children on the other.

Chungking! End of the journey for my companions. The start of the journey for me, the start of another life. I had no friendship for it as I looked at the steep gorges of the swirling rivers. The city was built on high cliffs quite thickly clothed with houses. From where we stood it appeared to be an island, but we knew better. We knew that it was not so, but was surrounded on three sides by the waters of the rivers Yangtse and Chialing. At the foot of the cliffs, washed by the water, was a long wide strand of sand, tapering off to a point where the rivers met. This was to be a spot well known to me in later months. Slowly we mounted our horses and moved forward. As we got nearer we saw that steps were everywhere and we had a sharp pang of homesickness as we climbed the seven hundred and eighty steps of the street of steps. It reminded us of the Potala. And so we came to Chungking.

CHAPTER TWO

Chungking

WE went along past the shops with brilliantly lighted windows, and in those windows were materials and goods of a kind which we had never seen before. Some of them we had seen pictured in magazines which had been brought to Lhasa over the Himalaya from India, and before reaching India from the U.S.A., that fabled land. A young Chinese came hurtling towards us on the weirdest thing I had ever seen, an iron framework with two wheels, one in front, one behind. He looked at us and could not take his eyes away. Through this he lost control of the framework, the front wheel hit a stone, the thing turned sideways, and the rider went straight over the front wheel to land on his back. Some elderly Chinese lady was almost swept off her feet by him. She turned round and berated the poor fellow, who we considered had already suffered enough. He got up, looking remarkably foolish, and picked up his iron framework with the front wheel buckled. He put it across his shoulders and went on sadly down the hill, the street of steps. We thought we had come to a mad place, because everyone was acting most peculiarly. We went slowly along, marvelling at the goods in the shops, trying to decipher what price they would be, and what they were for, because although we had seen the magazines from America none of us had understood the slightest word, but had entertained ourselves with the pictures alone.

Further along we came upon the college which I was to attend. We stopped, and I went inside so that I could report my arrival. I have friends still in the hands of the Communists, and I do not intend to give any information whereby they can be identified because I used to be most intimately connected with the Young Tibetan Resistance Movement. We most actively resisted the Communists in Tibet. I entered, there were three steps. I went up these and into a room. Here there was a desk at which a young Chinese was sitting on one of those peculiar little platforms of wood, supported by four poles and with two more poles and a crossbar to support the back. What a lazy way of sitting, I thought, I could never manage like that! He looked quite a pleasant young fellow. He was dressed in blue linen as most of the Chinese were. He had a badge in his lapel which indicated that he was a servant of the college. At sight of me his eyes opened quite wide, his mouth started to open as well. Then he stood up and clasped his hands together while he bowed low. "I am one of the new students here," I said. "I have come from Lhasa, in Tibet, with a letter from the Abbot of the Potola Lamasery." And I proffered the long envelope which I had treasured so carefully during our journey, and which I protected from all the rigours of travel. He took it from me, and gave three bows, and then, "Venerable Abbot," he said, "will you sit down here until I return?" "Yes, I have plenty of time," I said, and I sat down in the lotus position. He looked embarrassed and fidgeted nervously with his fingers. He stepped from foot to foot and then swallowed. "Venerable Abbot," he said, "with all humility, and with the deepest respect, may I suggest that you get used to these chairs because we use them in this college." I rose to my feet and sat down most gingerly on one of those abominable contraptions. I thought —as I still think—I will try anything once! This thing seemed to me to be an instrument of torture. The young man went away and left me sitting. I fidgeted, and fidgeted. Soon pain appeared across my back, then I got a stiff neck and I felt thoroughly out of sorts with everything. Why, I thought, in this unfortunate country one cannot even sit properly as we did in Tibet, but here we have to be propped up from the ground. I tried to shift sideways and the chair creaked, groaned, and swayed, and after that I dared not move again for fear that the whole thing would collapse.

The young man returned, bowed to me again, and said, "The Principal will see you, Venerable Abbot. Will you come this way." He gestured with his hands and made for me to go ahead of him. "No," I said, "you lead the way. I don't know which way to go." He bowed again and took the lead. It all seemed so silly to me, some of these foreigners, they say they will show you the way and then they expect you to lead them. How can you lead when you just don't know which way to go? That was my point of view and it still is. The young man in blue led me along a corridor and then knocked at the door of a room near the end. With another bow he opened the door for me and said, "The Venerable Abbot, Lobsang Rampa." With that he shut the door behind me and I was left in the room. There was an old man standing by the window, a very pleasant old man, bald and with a short beard, a Chinaman. Strangely, he was dressed in that awful style of clothing which I had seen before, that they call the western style. He had on a blue jacket and blue trousers and there was a thin white stripe going through. He had on a collar and a coloured tie, and I thought what a sad thing that such an impressive old gentleman has to get rigged up like that. "So you are Lobsang Rampa," he said. "I have heard a lot about you and I am honoured to accept you here as one of our students. I have had a letter about you in addition to the one you brought and I assure you that the previous training which you have had will stand you in very good stead. Your Guide, the Lama Mingyar Dondup, has written to me. I knew him well some years ago in Shanghai before I went to America. My name is Lee, and I am the Principal here."

I had to sit down and answer all sorts of questions to test my knowledge of academic subjects and my knowledge of anatomy. The things that mattered, or so it seemed to me, the Scriptures, he tested not at all.

"I am very pleased with your standard," he said, "but you are going to have to study quite hard because here, in addition to the Chinese system, we teach according to the American method of medicine and surgery, and you will have to learn a number of subjects which were not previously in your curriculum. I am qualified in the United States of America, and I have been entrusted by the Board of Trustees with training a number of young men in the latest American methods and co-relating these methods to suit conditions in China." He went on talking for quite a time, telling me of the wonders of American medicine and surgery, and of the methods used for diagnosis. He went on, "Electricity, Magnetism, Heat, Light and Sound, all these subjects you will have to master in addition to the very thorough culture which your Guide has given you." I looked at him in horror. The first two, Electricity and Magnetism, meant nothing to me. I had not the vaguest idea what he was talking about. But Heat, Light and Sound, well, I thought, any fool knows about those; you use heat to heat your tea, you use light with which to see, and sound when you speak. So what else is there to study about them? He added, "I am going to suggest that as you are used to hard work, you should study twice as hard as anyone else, and take two courses together, take what we term the Pre-medical Course at the same time as the Medical Training. With your years of experience in study you should be able to do this. In two days' time we have a new Medical Class starting." He turned away and rustled through his papers. Then he picked up what from pictures I recognised as a fountain pen—the very first I had ever seen—he muttered to himself, "Lobsang Rampa, special training in Electricity and in Magnetism. See Mr. Wu. Make a note he gets special attention." He put down his pen, carefully blotted what he had written, and stood up. I was most interested to see that he used paper for blotting. We used carefully dried sand. But he was standing up looking at me. "You are well

35

advanced in some of your studies," he said. "From our discussion I should say that you are even in advance of some of our own doctors, but you will have to study those two subjects of which, at present, you have no knowledge." He touched a bell and said, "I will have you shown around and taken to the different departments so that you will have some impression to carry away with you this day. If you are in doubt, if you are uncertain, come to me, for I have promised the Lama Mingyar Dondup to help you to the full extent of my power." He bowed to me, and I touched my heart to him as I bowed back. The young man in the blue dress entered. The Principal spoke to him in Mandarin. He then turned to me and said, "If you will accompany Ah Fu, he will show you around our college, and answer any questions you may care to put." This time the young man turned and led the way out, carefully shutting the Principal's door behind him. In the corridor he said, "We must go to the Registrar first because you have to sign your name in a book." We went down the corridor and crossed a large hall with a polished floor. At the far side of it was another corridor. We went along it a few paces and then into a room where there was a lot of activity. Clerks were very busy apparently compiling lists of names, while other young men were standing before small tables writing their names in large books. The clerk who was guiding me said something to another man who disappeared into an office adjoining the larger office. Shortly after, a short, squat Chinaman came out, beaming. He wore extremely thick glasses and he, too, was dressed in the Western style. "Ah," he said, "Lobsang Rampa. I have heard such a lot about you." He held out his hand to me. I looked at it. I did not know what he wanted me to give him. I thought perhaps he was after money. The guide with me whispered, "You must shake his hand in the Western style." "Yes, you must shake my hand in the Western style," the short, fat man said "We are going to use that system here." So I took his

36

hand and squeezed it. "Ow!" he said, "You are crushing my bones." I said, "Well, I don't know what to do. In Tibet we touch our hearts, like this." And I demonstrated. He said, "Oh, yes, but times are changing. We use this system. Now shake my hand properly, I will show you how." And he demonstrated. So I shook his hand, and I thought, how utterly stupid this is. He said, "Now you must sign your name to show that you are a student with us." He roughly brushed aside some of the young men who were at the books, and wet his finger and thumb, then he turned over a big ledger. "There," he said, "will you sign your full name and rank there?" I picked up a Chinese pen and signed my name at the head of the page. "Tuesday Lobsang Rampa," I wrote, "Lama of Tibet. Priest-Surgeon Chakpori Lamasery. Recognised Incarnation. Abbot Designate. Pupil of the Lama Mingyar Dondup." "Good!" said the short, fat Chinaman, as he peered down at my writing. "Good!" We shall get on. I want you to look round our place now. I want you to get an impression of all the wonders of Western science there are here. We shall meet again." With that he spoke to my guide, and the young fellow said, "Will you come with me, we will go along to the science room first." We went out and walked briskly across the compound and into another long building. Here there was glassware everywhere. Bottles, tubing, flasks—all the equipment that we had seen before only in pictures. The young man walked to a corner. "Now!" he exclaimed. "Here is something." And he fiddled about with a brass tube and put a piece of glass at the foot of it. Then he twisted a knob, peering into the brass tube. "Look at that!" he exclaimed. I looked. I saw the culture of a germ. The young man was looking at me anxiously. "What! aren't you astounded?" he said. "Not at all," I replied. "We had a very good one at the Potala Lamasery given to the Dalai Lama by the Government of India. My Guide, the Lama Mingyar Dondup, had free access to it and I used it often." "Oh!" replied the young man, and he looked most disappointed. "Then I will show you something else." And he led the way out of the building and into another. "You are going to live at the Lamasery of the Hill," he said, "but I thought you would like to see the very latest facilities which are enjoyed by students who are going to live in." He opened a room door and I saw first whitewashed walls, and then my fascinated gaze fell upon a black iron frame with a lot of twisted wire stretching from side to side. "What is that?" I exclaimed. "I have never seen anything like that before." "That," he said, with tones full of pride, "that is a bed. We have six of them in this building, the most modern things of all." I looked. I had never seen anything like it. "A bed," I said. "What do they do with the thing?" "Sleep on it," he replied. "It is a very comfortable thing indeed. Lie on it and see for yourself." I looked at him, I looked at the bed, and I looked at him again. Well, I thought, I must not show cowardice in front of one of these Chinese clerks and so I sat down on the bed. It creaked and groaned beneath me, it sagged, and I felt that I was going to fall on the floor. I jumped up hastily, "Oh, I am too heavy for it," I said. The young man was trying to conceal his laughter. "Oh, that is what it is meant to do," he answered. "It's a bed, a spring bed." And he flung himself full length on it, and bounced. No, I would not do that, it was a terrible looking thing. I had always slept on the ground, and the ground was good enough for me. The young man bounced again, and bounced right off and landed with a crash on the ground. Serves him right, I thought, as I helped him to his feet. "That is not all I have to show you," he said. "Look at this." He led me across to a wall where there was a small basin which could have been used for making tsampa for, perhaps, half a dozen monks. "Look at it," he said, "wonderful, isn't it?" I looked at it. It conveyed nothing to me, I could see no use in it. It had a hole in the bottom. "That's no good," I said. "It has a hole in

38

it. Couldn't make tea in that." He laughed, he was really amused at that. "That," he said, "is something even newer than the bed. Look!" He put out his hand and touched a lump of metal which was sticking up from one side of the white bowl. To my utter stupefaction water came out of the metal. Water! "It's cold," he said. "Quite cold. Look." And he put his hand in it. "Feel it," he said. So I did. It was water, just like river water. Perhaps a bit staler, it smelled a bit staler than river water, but—water from a piece of metal. Whoever heard of it! He put his hand out and picked up a black thing and pushed it in the hole, in the bottom of the basin. The water tinkled on; soon it filled the basin but did not overflow, it was going somewhere else, through a hole somewhere, but it wasn't falling on the floor. The young man touched the lump of metal again and the flow of water stopped. He put his two hands in the basinful of water and swirled it about. "Look," he said, "lovely water. You don't have to go out and dig it out of a well any more." I put my hands in the water and swirled as well. It was quite a pleasant sensation, not having to get down on hands and knees to reach into the depths of some river. Then the young man pulled a chain and the water rushed away gurgling like an old man at the point of death. He turned round and picked up what I had thought was somebody's short cloak. "Here," he said, "use this." I looked at him and I looked at the piece of cloth he had handed me. "What is this for?" I said, "I am fully dressed." He laughed again. "Oh, no, you wipe your hands on this," he said. "Like this," and he showed me. He passed the cloth back. "Wipe them dry," he said. So I did, but I marvelled because the last time I had seen women to speak to in Tibet they would have been very glad of such a piece of cloth to make something useful from it, and here we were spoiling it by wiping our hands on it. Whatever would my mother have said if she could have seen me!

By now I really was impressed. Water from metal.

Basins with holes in that could be used. The young man led the way quite jubilantly. We went down some steps and into a room which was underground. "Here," he said, "this is where we keep bodies, men and women." He flung open a door and there, on stone tables, were bodies all ready to be dissected. The air smelt strongly of strange chemicals which had been used to prevent the bodies from decaying. At the time I had no idea at all of what they were, because in Tibet bodies would keep a very long time without decay because of the cold dry atmosphere. Here, in sweltering Chungking, they had to be injected almost as soon as they were dead, so that they could be preserved for the few months which we students would need to dissect them. He moved a cabinet, and opened it. "Look," he said. "The latest surgical equipment from America. For cutting up bodies, for cutting off arms and legs. Look!" I looked at all those gleaming pieces of metal, all the glasswork, and all the chromium, and I thought, well, I doubt if they can do things any better than we did in Tibet.

After I had been in the college buildings for about three hours I made my way back to my companions who were sitting somewhat anxiously in the quadrangle of the building. I told them what I had seen, what I had been doing. Then I said, "Let us look around this city, let us see what sort of a place it is. It looks very barbaric to me, the stench and the noise is terrible." So we got on our horses again, and made our way out, and looked at the street of steps with all the shops. We dismounted so that we could go and look, one by one, at the remarkable things there were for sale. We looked down streets, down one street at the end of which there seemed to be no further road, it seemed to end abruptly at a cliff. It intrigued us so we walked down and saw that it dipped steeply and there were further steps leading down to the docks. As we looked we could see great cargo vessels, high-stemmed, junks, their lateen sails flapping idly against the masts in the idle breeze which played at the foot of the cliff. Coolies were loading some, going aboard at a jog-trot with long bamboo poles on their shoulders. At each end of the poles were loads carried in baskets. It was very warm, and we were sweltered. Chungking is noted for its sultry atmosphere. Then, as we walked along leading our horses mist came down from the clouds, and then it came up from the river, and we were groping about as if in darkness. Chungking is a high city, high and somewhat alarming. It was a steep stony city with almost two million inhabitants. The streets were precipitous, so precipitous indeed that some of the houses appeared to be caves in the mountainside, while others seemed to jut out and to overhang the abyss. Here every foot of soil was cultivated, jealously guarded, tended. There were strips and patches growing rice or a row of beans or a patch of corn, but nowhere was ground wasted or idle. Everywhere blue-clad figures were bent over, as if they were born that way, picking weeds with tired fingers. The higher class of people lived in the valley of Kialing, a suburb of Chungking, where the air was, by Chinese standards, though not by ours, healthy, where the shops were better and the ground more fertile. Where there were trees and pleasant streams. This was no place for coolies, this was for the prosperous business man, for the professional, and for those of independent means. The Mandarin and those of high caste lived here. Chungking was a mighty city, the biggest city any of us had ever seen, but we were not impressed.

It suddenly dawned upon us that we were very hungry. We were completely out of food, so there was nothing to do but go to an eating place, and eat as the Chinese did. We went to a place with a garish sign which said that they could provide the best meal in Chungking and without delay. We went and sat down at a table. A blue-clad figure came to us and asked what we would have. "Have you tsampa?" I said. "Tsampa!" he replied. "Oh, no, that must be one of those Western dishes. We have nothing like that."

41

"Well, what have you?" I said. "Rice, noodles, shark's fins, eggs." "All right," I said, "we will have rice balls, noodles, shark's fin, and bamboo shoot. Hurry up." He hurried away and in moments was back with the food we wanted. About us others were eating and we were horrified at the chatter and noise they were making. In Tibet, in the lamaseries, it was an inviolable rule that those who were eating did not talk because that was disrespectful to food and the food might retaliate by giving one strange pains inside. In the lamaseries when one ate, a monk always read aloud the Scriptures and we had to listen as we ate. Here there were conversations going on around us of an extremely light type. We were shocked and disgusted. We ate looking at our plates the whole time in the manner prescribed by our order. Some of the talk was not so light because there was much surreptitious discussion about the Japanese and the trouble they had been making in various parts of China. At that time I was quite ignorant of it. We were not impressed, though, by anything to do with the eating place nor with Chungking. This meal was notable only for this; it was the first meal that I ever had to pay for. After we had had it we went out and found a place in a courtyard of some municipal building where we could sit and talk. We had stabled our horses to give them a much needed rest and where they could be fed and watered, because on the morrow my companions were going to set out once again for home, for Tibet. Now, in the manner of tourists the world over they were wondering what they could take back to their friends in Lhasa, and I too was wondering what I could send to the Lama Mingyar Dondup. We discussed it, and then as if on a common impulse we got to our feet and we walked again to the shops and made our purchases. After that we walked to a small garden where we sat and talked and talked. It was dark now. The evening was upon us. The stars began to shine vaguely through the slight haze, for the fog had gone leaving just a haze. Once again we rose to our feet and and went again in search of food. This time it was seafood, food which we had never had before and which tasted almost alien to us, most unpleasant, but the main thing was that it was food, because we were hungry. With our supper completed we left the eating place and went to where our horses were stabled. They seemed to be waiting for us and whinnied with pleasure at our approach. They were looking quite fresh, they felt quite fresh too as we got upon them. I was never a good horseman and certainly I preferred a tired horse to a rested one. We rode out into the street and took the road to Kialing.

We left the city of Chungking and we passed through the outskirts of that city on the road to where we were going to stay the night, to the lamasery which was going to be my home by night. We branched to the right and went up the side of a wooded hill. The lamasery was of my own order and it was the nearest approach to going home to Tibet as I entered and went into the temple in time for the service. The incense was wafted round in clouds and the deep voices of the older monks and the higher voices of the acolytes brought a sharp pang of homesickness to me. The others seemed to know how I felt for they were silent and they left me to myself. For a time I stayed in my place after the service had ended. I thought, and thought. I thought of the first time I had entered a lamasery temple after a hard feat of endurance, when I was hungry and sick at heart. Now I was sick at heart, perhaps sicker at heart than I had been the time before, for then I had been too young to know much about life, but now I felt I knew too much of life, and of death. After a time the aged abbot in charge of the lamasery crept softly to my side. "My brother," he said, "it is not good to dwell too much upon the past when the whole of the future is before one. The service is ended, my brother, soon it will be time for another service. Will you not go to your bed for there is much to be done on the morrow." I rose to my feet without speaking and accompanied him to where I was to sleep. My companions had already retired. I passed them, still forms rolled in their blankets. Asleep? Perhaps. Who knows? Perhaps they were dreaming of the journey they had again to undertake and of the pleasurable re-union which they would have at the end of that journey in Lhasa. I, too, rolled myself in my blanket, and lay down. The shadows of the moon lengthened and became long before I slept.

I was awakened by the sound of temple trumpets, by gongs. It was time to rise and to attend the service once again. The service must come before the meal, but I was hungry. Yet after the service with food before me I had no appetite. Mine was a light meal, a very light meal because I was feeling sick at heart. My companions ate well, disgustingly well, I thought, but they were trying to get reinforced for the journey back which they were this day to commence. With our breakfast over we walked around a little. None of us said much. There did not seem much which we could say. Then at last I said, "Give this letter and this gift to my Guide, the Lama Mingyar Dondup. Tell him I will write to him often. Tell him that you can see how much I miss his company and his guidance." I fiddled about inside my robe. "And this," I said as I produced a package, "this is for the Inmost One. Give it also to my Guide, he will see that it is conveyed to the Dalai Lama." They took it from me and I turned aside quite overcome with emotion that I did not want the others to see, I did not want them to see me, a high lama, so affected. Fortunately they too were quite distressed because a sincere friendship had sprung up between us, notwithstanding—according to Tibetan standards—the difference in our rank. They were sorry for the parting, sorry that I was being left in this strange world which they hated while they were going back to beloved Lhasa. We walked for a time amid the trees looking at the little flowers carpeting the ground, listening to the birds in the branches, watching the light clouds overhead. Then the time had come. Together we walked back to the old Chinese lamasery nestling amid the trees on the hill overlooking Chungking, overlooking the rivers. There wasn't much to say, there wasn't much to do. We fidgeted a bit and felt depressed. We went to the stables. Slowly my companions saddled their horses and took the bridle of mine, mine which had brought me so faithfully from Lhasa, and which now—happy creature—was going back to Tibet. We exchanged a few words more, a very few words, then they got on their horses and moved off towards Tibet leaving me standing, gazing down the road after them. They got smaller and smaller. They disappeared from my sight around a bend. A little cloud of dust which had been occasioned by their passing subsided, the clip-clop of their horses' hooves died in the distance. I stood thinking of the past and dreading the future. I do not know how long I stood in silent misery but I was brought from my despondent reverie by a pleasant voice which said, "Honourable Lama, will you not remember that in China there are those who will be friends with you? I am at your service, Honourable Lama of Tibet, fellow student of Chungking." I turned slowly and there, just behind me, was a pleasant young Chinese monk. I think he rather wondered what my attitude would be to his approach because I was an abbot, a high lama, and he was just a Chinese monk. But I was delighted to see him. He was Huang, a man whom I was later proud to call a friend. We soon got to know each other and I was particularly glad to know that he too was going to be a medical student, starting on the morrow, as was I. He, too, was going to study those remarkable things, Electricity and Magnetism. He was, in fact, to be in both of those courses which I was going to study, and we got to know each other well. We turned and walked back towards the entrance of the lamasery. As we passed the portals another Chinese monk came forward and said "We have to report to the

45

college. We have to sign a register." "Oh, I have done all that," I said, "I did it yesterday." "Yes Honourable Lama," the other replied. "But this is not the studentship register which you signed with us, it is a fraternity register because in the college we are all going to be brothers as they are in American colleges." So together we turned down the path once more, along the lamasery path, through the trees, the path carpeted with flowers, and we turned into the main road from Kialing to Chungking. In the company of these young men who were of much the same age as I, the journey did not seem so long nor so miserable. Soon, once again, we came to the buildings which were to be our day-time home and we went in. The young clerk in the blue linen dress was really pleased to see us. He said, "Ah, I was hoping you would call, we have an American journalist here who speaks Chinese. He would very much like to meet a high lama of Tibet."

He led us along the corridor again and into another room, a room which I had not previously entered. It appeared to be some sort of reception room because a lot of young men were sitting about talking to young women, which I thought rather shocking. I knew very little about women in those days. A tall young man was sitting in a very low chair. He was, I should say, about thirty years of age. He rose as we entered and touched his heart to us in the Eastern way. I of course touched mine in return. We were introduced to him, and then, for some reason, he put out his hand. This time I was not unprepared and I took it, and shook it in the approved manner. He laughed, "Ah, I see that you are mastering the ways of the West which are being introduced to Chungking." "Yes," I said, "I have got to the stage of sitting in the perfectly horrible chairs and of shaking hands." He was quite a nice young fellow, and I know his name still; he died in Chungking some time ago. We walked into the grounds and sat down on a low stone wall where we talked for quite a time. I told him of Tibet, of our customs.

I told him much about my life in Tibet. He told me of America. I asked him what he was doing in Chungking, a man of his intelligence living in a sweltering place like that when apparently there was no particular reason for him to. He said that he was preparing a series of articles for a very famous American magazine. He asked if he could mention me in it, and I said, "Well, I would rather that you did not because I am here for a special purpose, to study to progress, and to use this as a jumping-off point for further journeys into the West. I would rather wait until I have done something notable, something worthy of mention. And then," I went on, "then I will get in touch with you and give you this interview which you so much want." He was a decent young fellow and understood my point. We were soon on quite friendly terms; he spoke Chinese passably well and we had no particular difficulty in understanding each other. He walked with us part of the way back to the lamasery. He said, "I would very much like sometime, if it can be arranged, to visit the temple and to take part in a service. I am not of your religion," he said, "but I respect it, and I would like to pay my respects in your temple." "All right," I answered, "you shall come to our temple. You shall take part in our service and you will be welcome, that I promise." With that we parted company because we had so much to do preparing for the morrow, the morrow when I was to begin this fresh career as a student—as if I had not been studying all my life! Back in the lamasery I had to sort out my things, see to my robes which had been travel-stained; I was going to wash them because, according to our custom, we attend to our own clothing, to our own robes, to our own personal matters, and did not employ servants to do our dirty work for us. I was also later going to wear the clothes of a Chinese student, blue clothes, because my own lamastic robes attracted too much attention and I did not want to be singled out for publicity, I wanted to study in peace. In addition to the usual things such as clothes-washing we had our services to attend, and as a leading lama I had to take my share in the administration of these services because, although during the day I was to be a student, yet at the lamasery I was still a high-ranking priest with the obligations that went with that office. So the day drew to an end, the day which I thought was never going to end, the day when, for the first time in my life, I was completely and utterly cut off from my own people.

In the morning—it was a warm sunny morning—Huang and I set off down the road again to a new life, this time as medical students. We soon covered the short journey and went into the college grounds where there seemed to be hundreds of others milling around a notice board. We carefully read all the notices and found our names were together so that at all times we should be studying together. We pushed our way past others still reading, and made our way to the classroom which had been indicated to us. Here we sat down, rather marvelling—or I did—at all the strangeness of the fittings, the desks, and all that. Then, after what seemed to be an eternity of time, others came in, in small groups, and took their places. Eventually a gong sounded somewhere and a Chinaman entered, and said, "Good morning, gentlemen." We all rose to our feet because the regulations said that that was the approved method of showing respect, and we replied, "Good morning," back to him. He said he was going to give us some written papers and we were not to be discouraged by our failures because his task was to find out what we did not know, not how much we knew. He said that until he could find the exact standard of each of us he would not be able to assist us. The papers would deal with everything, various questions all mixed up, a veritable Chinese broth of knowledge dealing with Arithmetic, Physics, Anatomy, everything relating to medicine and surgery and science, and the subjects which were necessary to enable us to study medicine, surgery and science to higher levels. He gave us clearly to understand

48

that if we did not know how to answer a question then we could put down that we had not studied to that point but give, if we could, some information so that he could assess the exact point at which our knowledge ended. Then he rang the bell. The door opened and in came two attendants laden with what seemed to be books. They moved amongst us and distributed these books. They were not books, actually, but sheaves of questions on paper and many sheets of paper upon which we were to write. Then the other one came and distributed pencils. We were going to use pencils and not brushes on this occasion. So, then we set to, reading through the questions, one by one, answering them as best we could. We could see by the lecturer's aura, or at least I could, that he was a genuine man and that his only interest was to help us.

My Guide and Tutor, the Lama Mingyar Dondup, had given me very highly specialized training. The result of the papers which we were given in about two days' time showed that in very many subjects I was well in advance of my fellow students, but it showed that I had no knowledge whatever of Electricity or Magnetism. Perhaps a week after that examination we were in a laboratory where we were to be given a first demonstration because, like me, some of the others had no idea of the meaning of those two dreadful sounding words. The lecturer had been giving us a talk about electricity and he said, "Now, I will give you a practical demonstration of the effects of electricity, a harmless demonstration." He handed me two wires and said, "Hold these, will you, hold them tightly until I say, 'let go'." I thought that he was asking me to assist him in his demonstration (he was!) and so I held the wires, although I was rather perturbed because his aura showed that he was contemplating some form of treachery. I thought, well perhaps I am misjudging him, he's not a very nice fellow anyhow. He turned and walked quickly away from me to his own demonstration table. There he pressed a switch. I saw light coming from the wire and I saw the aura of the lecturer betray amazement. He appeared to be intensely surprised. "Hold them tighter," he said. So I did. I squeezed the wires. The lecturer looked at me and really rubbed his eyes. He was astounded, that was obvious to everyone, even anyone without the ability to see the aura. It was obvious that this lecturer had never had such a surprise before. The other students looked on in open-mouthed wonder. They could not understand what it was all about. They had no idea at all what was intended. Quickly the lecturer came back to me after switching off and took the two wires from me. He said, "There must be something wrong, there must be a disconnection." He took the two wires in his hand and went back to the table with them. One wire was in his left hand, the other was in his right. Still holding them he stretched forth a finger and flicked on the switch. Then he erupted into a tremendous "Yow! Switch off, it's killing me!" At the same time his body was knotted up as if all his muscles were tied and paralysed. He continued to yell and scream and his aura looked like the setting sun. "How very interesting," I thought, "I have never seen anything as pretty as that in the human aura!"

The continued shrieks of the lecturer soon brought people running in. One man took a glance at him and rushed to the table and switched off the switch. The poor lecturer dropped to the floor, perspiring freely and shaking. He looked a sorry sight; his face had a pale greenish tinge to it. Eventually he stood up clasping the edge of the desk. "You did that to me." I replied, "I? I haven't done a thing. You told me to hold the wires and I held them, then you took them from me and you looked as if you were going to die." He said, "I can't understand it. I can't understand it." I answered, "What can't you understand? I held the things, what are you talking about?" He looked at me: "Didn't you really feel anything? Didn't you feel a tingle or anything?" "Well," I said, "I felt just a pleasant bit of warmth, nothing more. Why, what should I feel?" Another lecturer, the one who had switched off the current said, "Will you try it again?" I said, "Of course I will, as many times as you like." So he handed me the wires. He said, "Now I am going to switch on. Tell me what happens." He pressed the switch, and I said, "Oh, it's just a pleasant bit of warmth. Nothing to worry about at all. It's just as if I had my hands fairly close to a fire." He said, "Squeeze it tighter." And I did so, I actually squeezed it until the muscles stood out on the backs of my hands. He and the previous lecturer looked at each other, and the current was switched off. Then one of them took the two wires from me and put cloth around them, and he held them lightly in his hands. "Switch on," he said to the other. So the other lecturer switched on, and the man with the wires wrapped in cloth in his hands soon dropped it. He said, "Oh, it's still on." In dropping the two wires fell free of the cloth and touched. There was a vivid blue flash, and a lump of molten metal jumped from the end of the wire. "Now you have blown the fuses," said one, and he went off to do a repair somewhere.

With the current restored they went on with their lecture about Electricity. They said they were trying to give me two hundred and fifty volts as a shock to show what electricity could do. I have a peculiarly dry skin and two hundred and fifty volts hurt me not at all. I can put my hands on the mains and be quite unaware of whether they are on or not. The poor lecturer was not of that type at all, he was remarkably susceptible to electric currents. In the course of the lecture they said, "In America if a man commits murder, or if the lawyers say that he is guilty of murder, the man is killed by electricity. He is strapped to a chair, and the current is applied to his body and it kills him." I thought how very interesting. I wonder what they would do with me, although I have no desire to try it seriously.

51

CHAPTER THREE

Medical Days

A DANK, grey fog came down from the hills above Chungking, blotting out the houses, the river, the masts of the ships down below, turning the lights in the shops to orange-yellow blurs, deadening the sounds, perhaps even improving the appearance of part of Chungking. There was the slithering sound of footsteps and a bent old man came dimly into sight through the fog, and was as quickly lost to view again. It was strangely silent here, the only sounds were muffled sounds. The fog was as a thick blanket deadening all. Huang and I had finished our classes for the day, and it was now late evening. We had decided to go out from the college, from the dissecting rooms, and get a breath of fresh air. Instead we had got this fog. I was feeling hungry; apparently so was Huang. The dampness had got into our bones and chilled us. "Let us go and have some food, Lobsang. I know a good place," said Huang. "All right," I answered. "I am always ready for something interesting. What have you got to show me?" "Oh, I want to show you that we in Chungking can live quite well in spite of what you say." He turned and led the way, or rather he turned and groped blindly till we reached the side of the street and were able to identify the shops. We went down the hill a little way, and then through an entrance which appeared to be remarkably like a cavern in the side of a mountain. Inside the air was even thicker than outside. People were smoking, belching great clouds of evil smelling fumes. It was almost the first time I had seen such a number of people smoking, and it was quite a novelty—a nauseating one—to see people with burning brands in their mouth, and smoke trickling out of their nostrils. One man attracted my fascinated gaze. He was producing smoke not just from his nostrils, but from his ears. I pointed him out to Huang. "Oh, him," he said, "he's stone deaf, you know. Had his ear-drums kicked in. It's quite a social asset with him. No eardrums to impede the smoke, so he sends it out of his nostrils and out of his ears too. He goes up to a foreigner and says, 'Give me a cigarette and I'll show you something you can't do'. Keeps him in smokes, that. Still that's nothing let's get on with the food. I'll order the meal," said Huang. "I am well known here and we shall get the best at the lowest price." It suited me fine. I had not eaten too well during the past few days, everything was so strange, and the food so utterly alien. Huang spoke to one of the waiters who made notes on a little pad, and then we sat down and talked. Food had been one of my problems. I could not obtain the type of food to which I was accustomed, and I had to eat, among other things, flesh and fish. To me, as a lama of Tibet, this was truly revolting, but I had been told by my seniors at the Potala in Lhasa that I would have to accustom myself to alien foods, and I had been given absolution from them for the type of food I should consume. In Tibet we, the priests, ate no meat but—this was not Tibet, and I had to continue to live in order to fulfil my allotted task. It was impossible to obtain the food I wanted, and so I had to eat the revolting messes brought me and pretend that I liked them.

Our lunch arrived. A half-tortoise surrounded with sea slugs, and followed by a dish of curried frogs with cabbage leaves around them. They were quite pleasant but I would have much preferred my own tsampa. So, making the best of things, I had my meal of curried frogs well supported with noodles and rice. We drank tea. One thing I have never touched in spite of all exhortations from those outside of Tibet have been intoxicating liquors. Never, never, never. In our belief there is nothing worse than these intoxicating

53

drinks, nothing worse than drunkenness. Drunkenness, we consider, is the most vicious sin of all because when the body is sodden with drink the astral vehicle—the more spiritual part of one—is driven out of the physical and has to leave it as prey to any prowling entities. This is not the only life; the physical body is just one particular manifestation, the lowest manifestation, and the more one drinks, the more one harms one's body in other planes of existence. It is well known that drunkards see "pink elephants" and curious things which have no parallel in the physical world. These, we believe, are the manifestations of some evil entity, some entity who is trying to make the physical body do some harm. It is well known that those who are drunk are not "in possession of their right senses." So—I have not at any time touched intoxicating drinks, not even corn spirit, not even rice wine.

Lacquered duck is a very nice form of food—for those who like meat, that is. I much preferred bamboo shoots; these are unobtainable in the West, of course. The nearest substitute to it is a form of celery which grows in a certain European country. The English celery is quite different and is not so suitable. While discussing Chinese food it is possibly of some interest to say that there is no such dish as chop suey; that is just a name, a generic name for Chinese food, ANY Chinese food. If anyone wants a really good Chinese meal they should go to a first class all-Chinese restaurant and have ragout of mushroom and bamboo shoot. Then they should take a fish soup. After that, lacquered duck. You will not have a carving knife in the real Chinese restaurant, but the waiter will come along with a small hatchet and he will chop up the duck for you into suitably sized slices. When these are approved by you they will be wrapped up with a piece of young onion into a sandwich of unleavened bread. One picks up these small sandwiches and devours each at a mouthful. The meal should end with lotus leaves, or, if you prefer, lotus root. Some people prefer lotus seed, but whichever it is you will need adequate quantities of Chinese tea. This is the type of meal we had in that eating house so well known to Huang. The price was surprisingly reasonable and when eventually we rose to continue our journey we were in quite a blissful state of geniality, well padded, and well fortified with good food to go out again and face the fog. So—we made our way up the street, along the road to Kialing, and when we were part way along that road we turned right into the path leading up to our temple. It was service time when we got back. The Tablets were hanging limply against their poles there was no breeze, and the clouds of incense were just hanging motionless too. The Tablets are of red material with gold Chinese ideographs upon them. They were the Tablets of the Ancestors and were used in much the same way as tombstones are used to commemorate the dead in Western countries. We bowed to Ho Tai and Kuan Yin, the god of good living and the Goddess of compassion, and went our way into the dimly lit interior of the temple for our service. After which we were unable to face our evening meal, but instead rolled ourselves into our blankets and drifted off to sleep.

There was never any shortage of bodies for dissection. Bodies in Chungking at that time were a very easily obtained commodity. Later, when the war started, we were to have more corpses than we could deal with! But these, these which were obtained for dissection, we kept in an underground room which was carefully cooled. As soon as we could obtain a fresh body from the streets, or from a hospital, we used to inject into the groin a most powerful disinfectant that served to preserve the body for some months. It was quite interesting to go down into the basement and see the bodies on slabs, and to notice how invariably they were thin bodies. We used to have quite heated disputes as to which of us should have the thinnest. The fat bodies were a great trouble in dissecting, there was so much

55

labour with so little result. One could go on cutting and cutting, dissecting out a nerve or an artery and have to dissect away layer after layer of fatty tissues. Bodies were not in short supply at all. Frequently we had so many on hand that we kept them in tanks, in pickle, as we called it. Of course it was not always easy to smuggle a body into the hospital because some of the relatives had strong opinions about such things. In those days young babies who had died were abandoned in the streets, or those adults whose families were too poor to pay for a satisfactory funeral left them out in the streets under cover of darkness. We medical students, then, frequently went out in the early morning to pick the best looking bodies, and, of course, the leanest! We could have had a whole body to ourselves often we worked two to a cadaver, one doing the head, the other doing the feet. That was more companionable. Quite frequently we had our lunch in the dissecting room if we were studying for some examination. It was no uncommon thing to see a student with his food spread out on the stomach of a cadaver while his text book, which he was reading, would be propped up against the thigh. It never occurred to us at that time that we could obtain all sorts of curious complaints through infection from those dead bodies. Our Principal, Dr. Lee, had all the latest American ideas; in some ways he was almost a crank for copying the Americans, but no matter, he was a good man, one of the most brilliant Chinamen that I have met, and it was a pleasure to study with him. I learned a lot and passed many examinations; but I still maintain that I learned far more morbid anatomy from the Body Breakers of Tibet.

Our college and the attached hospital were at the far end of the road away from the docks along from the street of steps. In fine weather we had quite a good view across the river, across the terraced fields, because it was in a very prominent position, a prominent landmark, in fact. Toward the harbour in a more business section of the street was an old, old shop looking as if it were in the last stages of decay. The woodwork appeared to be worm-eaten, and the paint was flaking from the boards. The door was ramshackle and rickety. Above it there was a cut-out wooden figure of a gaudily painted tiger. It was so arranged that it arched its back over the entrance. Yawning jowls with ferocious looking teeth and claws which were realistic enough to strike terror into anyone's heart. This tiger was meant to show virility—it is an old Chinese emblem for virility. This shop was a beacon for rundown men, and for those who wished to have greater vigour with which to pursue their amusements. Women, too, went here to get certain compounds, extract of tiger, or extract of ginseng root, when they wanted to have children and for some reason apparently could not. Extract of tiger or extract of ginseng contained large quantities of substance which help men and women in such difficult times, substances which have only recently been discovered by Western science who hail it as a great triumph of commerce and research. The Chinese and the Tibetans did not know so much about modern research, and so they have had those compounds for three or four thousand years and have not boasted unduly about it. It is a fact that the West could learn so much from the East if the West was more co-operative. But—to return to this old shop with its fierce tiger carved and painted above it, with a window full of strange looking powders, mummies and bottles of coloured liquids. This was the shop of an old style medical practitioner where it was still possible to obtain powdered toad, the horns of antelope ground to powder to act as an aphrodisiac, and other strange concoctions. Not often in these poorer quarters did the patient go to the modern surgery of the hospital for treatment. Instead he went to this dirty old shop in much the same way as his father had done, and perhaps as his father's father before had done also. He took his complaints to the physician in charge, who sat looking like an owl with powerful lensed spectacles behind a brown wooden barrier. He would discuss his case and the symptoms, and the old physician would solemnly nod his head and with finger tips touching he would ponderously prescribe the necessary medicine. One convention was that the medicine had to be coloured according to a special code. That was an unwritten law from time before history. For a stomach complaint the medicine provided would be yellow, while the patient suffering from a blood or a heart disease would have red medicine. Those afflicted with bile or liver complaints, or even with excessively bad temper would have a green medicine. Patients who were suffering from eye troubles would have blue lotion. The interior of a person presented great problems regarding which colour to use. If a person had a pain inside and it was thought to be of intestinal origin the medicine would be brown. An expectant mother had only— so she was told—to take the pulverised flesh of a turtle and the baby would be born painlessly, easily, almost before she was aware of it, and so her day's work would not be interfered with. One injunction was "Go home, put an apron around you, between your legs, so that the baby shall not drop and strike the ground, and then swallow this pulverised flesh of a turtle!"

The old, unregistered Chinese doctor could advertise, and this he did in a most spectacular manner. Usually he had a large sign, an immense painted sign above his house, to show what a wonderful healer he was. Not only that, but in his waiting room and surgery would be found great medals and shields which wealthy and frightened patients had given him to testify to the miraculous way in which he, with coloured medicines, powders and potions, had cured them of unknown and unspecified diseases.

The poor dentist was not so lucky, the older style of dentist, that is. Most of the time he had no particular house in which to see patients, but he saw them in the street. The victim sat down on a box and the dentist carried out his examination, his poking and probing, in full view of an appreciative audience. Then, with a lot of strange manoeuvres and gesticulations, he would proceed to extract the faulty tooth. "Proceed" is the right term because if the patient was frightened or excessively noisy it was not always easy to do an extraction and at times the dentist would not hesitate to call upon bystanders to hold the struggling victim. There was no anaesthetic used. The dentist did not advertise as the doctors did with signs and shields and medals, but instead around his neck he wore strings of teeth which he had extracted. Whenever he had extracted a tooth, that tooth would be picked up, carefully cleaned, and a hole drilled through it. It would then be threaded on to a string to add one more testimony to the skill of the dentist who had pulled so many.

It used to annoy us considerably when patients on whom we had lavished much time and care, and to whom we had given the very latest treatment and prescribed expensive drugs, crept surreptitiously into the back entrance of the old Chinese doctor's premises for treatment by him. We claimed that we cured the patient. The quack claimed that he cured. But the patient said nothing, he was too glad to be free of his ill.

As we became more and more advanced in our studies and walked the wards of the hospital we had on frequent occasions to go out with a full qualified doctor to treat people in their own homes, to assist at operations. Sometimes we had to descend the cliffs to inaccessible places, perhaps to some place where some poor unfortunate had fallen over and shattered bones or lacerated flesh almost beyond repair. We had visits to those who had floating homes upon the rivers. In the Kialing river there are people who live on house-boats, or even rafts of bamboo covered with matting on which they erect little huts. These swayed and bobbed at the bank of the river, and, unless we were very careful, particularly at night, it was remarkably easy to miss one's footing or to stand firmly upon a loose piece of bamboo which merely sank beneath one. Then one was not at all cheered by the laughter of the inevitable crowd of small boys who always gathered on such unfortunate occasions. The old Chinese peasants were able to put up with an amazing amount of pain. They never complained and they were always grateful for what we could do for them. We used to go out of our way to help the old people, perhaps help to clean up their little hut, or prepare food for them, but with the younger generation things were not so pleasant. They were getting restive, they were getting strange ideas. The men from Moscow were circulating among them, preparing them for the advent of Communism. We knew it, but there was nothing we could do except to stand by and watch helplessly.

But before we became so qualified we had an enormous amount of study to do, study a whole diversity of subjects for as long as fourteen hours a day. Magnetism as well as Electricity, to quote just two. I well remember the first lecture I attended on Magnetism. Then it was a subject almost entirely unknown to me. It was perhaps as interesting in its way as that which I attended on Electricity. The lecturer was not really a very pleasant individual, but here is what happened.

Huang had pushed his way through the crowd to read the notices on the board to see where we should go for the next class. He started reading, then, "Hoy, Lobsang," he called across to me, "we've got a lecture on Magnetism this afternoon." We were glad to see that we were in the same class because we had formed a very sincere friendship. We walked out into the quadrangle, across and into a classroom next door to that devoted to Electricity. We entered. Inside there was a lot of equipment much the same, it seemed to us, as that dealing with Electricity proper. Coils of wire, strange pieces of metal bent roughly to a horse shoe shape. Black rods, glass rods, and various glass boxes containing what looked like water, and bits of wood and lead. We took our places and the lecturer came in and stalked ponderously to his table. He was a heavy man, heavy in body, heavy in mind. Certainly he had a very good opinion of his own abilities, a far greater opinion of his abilities than his colleagues had of them! He too had been to America, and whereas some of the others of the tutorial staff had returned knowing how little they really knew, this one was utterly convinced that he knew everything, that his own brain was infallible. He took his place and for some reason picked up a wooden hammer and rapped violently on his desk. "Silence!" he roared, although there had not been a sound. "We are going to do Magnetism, the first lecture for some of you on this absorbing subject," he said. He picked up one of the bars bent in the shape of a horse-shoe. "This," he said, "has a field around it." I immediately thought of grazing horses. He said, "I am going to show you how to outline the field of the magnet with iron dust. Magnetism," he went on, "will activate each particle of this iron which will then draw for itself the exact outline of the force which motivates it." I incautiously remarked to Huang who was sitting behind me, "But any fool can see it now, why tamper with it?" The lecturer jumped up in a furious temper. "Oh," he said, "the great lama from Tibet—who doesn't know the first thing about Magnetism or Electricity—can see a magnetic field, can he?" He stabbed a finger violently in my direction. "So, great lama, you can see this wonderful field can you? The only man in existence who can perhaps," he said sneeringly. I stood up. "Yes, Honourable Lecturer, I can see it very clearly," I said. "I can also see the lights around those wires." He took his wooden hammer again, and brought it down with a succession of resounding crashes on his desk. "You lie," he said, "no one can see it. If you are so clever come and draw it for me and then we will see what sort of a mess you make of it." I sighed wearily as

61

I went up to him, picked up the magnet and went to the blackboard with a piece of chalk. The magnet I put flat on the board then I drew around it the exact shape of the blue-ish light which I could see coming from the magnet. I drew, also, those lighter striations which were within the field itself. It was such a simple matter for me, I had been born with the ability, and I had had the ability increased in me by operations. There was absolutely dead silence when I had finished, and I turned round. The lecturer was watching me and his eyes were quite literally bulging. "You've studied this before," he said, "it's a trick!" "Honourable Lecturer," I replied, "until this day I have never seen one of these magnets." He said, "Well, I do not know how you do it, but that is the correct field. I still maintain that it is a trick. I still maintain that in Tibet you learned only trickery. I do not understand it." He took the magnet from me, covered it with a sheet of thin paper, and on to the paper he sprinkled fine iron dust, with a finger he tapped on the paper and the dust took up the exact shape of that which I had drawn on the blackboard. He looked at it, he looked at my drawing, and he looked back at the outline in the iron filings. "I still do not believe you, man from Tibet," he said. "I still think that it is a trick." He sat down wearily and propped his head in his hands, then, with explosive violence, he jumped up and shot out his hand to me again. "You!" he said, "you said that you could see the field of that magnet. You also said, 'And I can see the light around those wires'." "That is so," I replied, "I can, I can see them easily." "Right!" he shouted at me, "now we can prove you wrong, prove you are a fake." He wheeled round, knocking over his chair in his temper. He hurried to a corner, bent down and with a grunt picked up a box, with wires protruding in a coil from the top. He stood up and placed it on the table in front of me. "Now," he said, "now, here is a very interesting box known as a high-frequency box. You draw

62

the field of that for me and I will believe in you; there you are, you draw that field." He looked at me as if to say, "I'll dare you to." I said, "All right. It's simple enough. Let us put it nearer the blackboard, otherwise I shall be doing it by memory." He picked up one end of the table and I picked up the other and we moved it right up close to the blackboard. I took the chalk in my hand, and turned away to the board. "Oh," I said, "it's all gone." I looked in amazement because there were just wires, nothing else, no field. I turned towards him, his hand was on a switch. He had switched off the current, but there was a look of absolute stupefaction on his face. "So!" he said, "you really can see that! Well, well, how remarkable." He switched on again and said, "Turn away from me and tell me when it is on and when it is off." I turned away from him and I was able to tell him, "Off, on, off." He left it off then and sat in his chair in the attitude of a man whose faith has received a crushing blow. Then, abruptly, he said, "Class dismissed." Turning to me, "Not you. I want to speak to you alone." The others muttered with resentment. They had come for a lecture and they had found some interest, why should they be turned out now? He just shooed them out, taking one or two by the shoulders to hustle them more quickly. The lecturer's word was law. With the classroom emptied he said, "Now, tell me more of this. What sort of trick is it?" I said, "It is not a trick. It is a faculty with which I was born and which was strengthened by a special operation. I can see auras. I can see your aura. From it I know that you do not want to believe, you do not want to believe that anyone has an ability which you have not. You want to prove me wrong." "No," he said, "I do not want to prove you wrong. I want to prove that my own training, my own knowledge is right, and if you can see this aura then surely all that I have been taught is wrong." "Not at all," I replied. "I say that all your training goes to prove the existence of an aura, because from the very little that

I have already studied of Electricity in this college, it indicates to me that the human being is powered by electricity." "What utter nonsense!" he said. "What absolute heresy." And he jumped to his feet. "Come with me to the Principal. We will get this thing settled!"

Dr. Lee was sitting at his desk, busily engaged with the papers of the college. He looked up mildly as we entered, peering over the top of his glasses. Then he removed them to see us the more clearly. "Reverend Principal," bawled the lecturer, "this man, this fellow from Tibet says that he can see the aura and that we all have auras. He is trying to tell me that he knows more than I do, the Professor of Electricity and Magnetism." Dr. Lee mildly motioned for us to be seated, and then said, "Well, what is it precisely? Lobsang Rampa can see auras. That I know. Of what do you complain?" The lecturer absolutely gaped in astonishment. "But, Reverend Principal," he exclaimed, "do YOU believe in such nonsense, such heresy, such trickery?" "Most assuredly I do," said Dr. Lee, "for he comes of the highest in Tibet, and I have heard of him from the highest." Po Chu looked really crestfallen. Dr. Lee turned to me and said, "Lobsang Rampa, I will ask you to tell us in your own words about this aura. Tell us as if we knew nothing whatever about the subject. Tell us so that we may understand and perhaps profit from your specialised experience." Well, that was quite a different matter. I liked Dr. Lee, I liked the way he handled things. "Dr. Lee," I said, "when I was born it was with the ability to see people as they really were. They have around them an aura which betrays every fluctuation of thought, every variation in health, in mental or in spiritual conditions. This aura is the light caused by the spirit within. For the first couple of years of my life I thought everyone saw as I did, but I soon learned that that was not so. Then, as you are aware, I entered a lamasery at the age of seven and underwent special training. In that lamasery I was given a special operation to make me see

64

with even greater clarity than that which I had seen before, but which also gave me additional powers. In the days before history was," I went on, "man had a Third Eye. Through his own folly man lost the power to use that sight and that was the purpose of my training at the lamasery in Lhasa." I looked at them and saw that they were taking it in very well. "Dr. Lee," I went on, "the human body is surrounded first of all by a bluish light, a light perhaps an inch, perhaps two inches thick. That follows and covers the whole of the physical body. It is what we call the etheric body and is the lowest of the bodies. It is the connection between the astral world and the physical. The intensity of the blue varies according to a person's health. Then beyond the body, beyond the etheric body too, there is the aura. It varies in size enormously depending on the state of evolution of the person concerned, depending also upon the standard of education of the person, and upon his thoughts. Your own aura is the length of a man away from you," I said to the Principal, "the aura of an evolved man. The human aura whatever its size, is composed of swirling bands of colours, like clouds of colours drifting on the evening sky. They alter with a person's thoughts. There are zones on the body, special zones, which produce their own horizontal bands of colour. Yesterday," I said, "when I was working in the library I saw some pictures in a book on some Western religious belief. Here there were portrayed figures which had auras around their heads. Does this mean that the people of the West whom I had thought inferior to us in development can see auras, while we of the East cannot? These pictures of the people of the West," I carried on, "had auras only around their heads. But I can see not merely around the head, but around the whole body and around the hands, the fingers and the feet. It is a thing which I have always seen." The Principal turned to Po Chu. "There, you see, this is the information which I had before. I knew that Rampa had this power. He used this power on behalf of the leaders of Tibet. That is why he is studying with us so that, it is hoped, he can assist in the developing of a special device which will be of the greatest benefit to mankind as a whole in connection with the detection and cure of disease. What caused you to come here to-day?" he asked. The lecturer was looking very thoughtful. He replied, "We were just commencing practical Magnetism, and before I could show anything, as soon as I spoke about fields, this man said that he could see the fields around the magnet which I knew to be utterly fantastic. So I invited him to demonstrate upon the blackboard. To my astonishment," he went on, "he was able to draw the field on the blackboard, and he was able also to draw the current field of a high frequency transformer, but when it was switched off he saw nothing. I am sure it was a trick." He looked defiantly at the Principal. "No," said Dr. Lee, "indeed it was no trick. It was no trick at all. For this is known to me as the truth. Some years ago I met his Guide, the Lama Mingyar Dondup, one of the cleverest men in Tibet, and he, out of the goodness of his heart, underwent certain tests, out of friendship for me, and he proved that he could do the same as can Lobsang Rampa. We were able—that is a special group of us—to make some serious researches into the matter. But, unfortunately, prejudice, conservatism, and jealousy prevented us from publishing our findings. It is a thing which I have regretted ever since."

There was silence for a time. I thought how good it was of the Principal to declare his faith in me. The lecturer was looking really gloomy as if he had received an unexpected, unwelcome setback. He said, "If you have this power, why are you studying medicine?" I replied, "I want to study medicine and I want to study science as well so that I may assist in the preparation of a device similar to that which I saw in the Chang Tang Highlands of Tibet." The Principal broke in, "Yes, I know that you were one of the men who went on that expedition. I should

like to know more about that device." "Some time ago,"
I said, "at the instigation of the Dalai Lama a small party
of us went upwards into a hidden valley in the mountain
ranges in the Chang Tang Highlands. Here we found a city
dating back to long before recorded history, a city of a
bygone race, a city partly buried in the ice of a glacier, but
where the glacier had melted in the hidden valley, where
it was warm, the buildings and the devices contained in the
buildings were intact. One such apparatus was a form of
box into which one could look and see the human aura,
and from that aura, from the colours, from the general
appearance, they could deduce the state of health of a
person. More, they could see if a person was likely to be
afflicted in the flesh by any disease because the probabili-
ties showed in the same aura before it was manifest in the
flesh. In the same way, the germs of coryza show in the
aura long before they manifest in the flesh as a common
cold. It is a far easier matter to cure a person when they
are only just tinged with a complaint. The complaint, the
disease, can then be eradicated before it obtains a hold."
The Principal nodded and said, "This is most interesting.
Go on." I went on: "I visualize a modern version of that
old apparatus. I would like to assist in the preparation of
a similar device so that even the most non-clairvoyant
doctor or surgeon could look through this box and could
see the aura of a person in colour. He could also have a
matching chart and with that chart he would be able to
know what was actually wrong with the person. He would
be able to diagnose without any difficulty or inaccuracy at
all." "But," said the lecturer, "you are too late. We have
X-rays already!" "X-rays," said Dr. Lee. "Oh, my dear
fellow, they are useless for a purpose such as this. They
merely show grey shadows of the bones. Lobsang Rampa
does not want to show the bones, he wants to show the
life-force of the body itself. I understand precisely what he
means and I am sure that the biggest difficulty with which

67

he will be confronted will be prejudice and professional jealousy." He turned to me again, "But how could one help in mental complaints with such a device?" "Reverend Principal," I said, "if a person has split personality the aura shows very clearly indeed because it shows a dual aura, and I maintain that with suitable apparatus the two auras could be pushed into one—perhaps by high frequency electricity."

Now I am writing this in the West and I am finding that there is much interest in these matters. Many medical men of the highest eminence have expressed interest but invariably they say that I must not mention their name as it would prejudice their reputation! These further few remarks may be of interest: have you ever seen power cables during a slight haze? If so, particularly in mountain areas, you will have seen a corona round the wires. That is, a faint light encircling the wires. If your sight is very good you will have seen the light flicker, wane and grow, wane and grow, as the current coursing through the wires alters in polarity. That is much the same as the human aura. The old people, our great, great, great-ancestors, evidently could see auras, or see haloes, because they were able to paint them on pictures of saints. That, surely, cannot be ascribed by any one as imagination because if it was imagination only why paint it on the head, why paint it on the head where there actually is a light? Modern science has already measured the waves of a brain, measured the voltage of a human body. There is, in fact, one very famous hospital where research was undertaken years ago into X-rays. The researchers found that they were taking pictures of a human aura, but they did not understand what they were taking, nor did they care, because they were trying to photograph bones, not colours on the outside of a body, and they looked upon this aura photography as an unmitigated nuisance. Tragically the whole of the matter relating to aura photography was shelved, while they progressed with X-rays which, in my quite humble opinion, is the wrong way. I am utterly confident that with a little research doctors and surgeons could be provided with the most wonderful aid of all towards curing the sick. I visualise—as I did many years ago—a special apparatus which any doctor could carry with him in his pocket, and then he could produce it and view a patient through it in much the same way as one takes a piece of smoked glass to look at the sun. With this device he could see the patient's aura, and by the striations of colour, or by irregularities in outline, he could see exactly what was wrong with the patient. That is not the most important thing, because it does not help to merely know what is wrong with a person, one needs to know how to cure him, and this he could do so easily with the device I have in mind, particularly in the case of those with mental afflictions.

CHAPTER FOUR

Flying

IT was a warm, sultry evening, with hardly a breeze. The clouds above the cliff upon which we were walking were perhaps two hundred feet above us, glowering cloud masses which reminded me of Tibet as they towered into fantastic shapes as imaginary mountain ranges. Huang and I had had a hard day in the dissecting rooms. Hard, because the cadavers there had been kept a long time, and the smell from them was just terrible. The smell of the decaying bodies, the smell of the antiseptic, and the other odours had really exhausted us. I wondered why I had ever had to come away from Tibet where the air was pure, and where men's thoughts were pure, too. After a time we had had enough of the dissecting rooms and we had washed and gone out to this cliff top. It was good, we thought, to walk in the evening and look upon nature. We looked upon other things as well because, by peering over the edge of the cliff, we could see the busy traffic on the river beneath. We could see the coolies loading ship, eternally carrying their heavy bales with a long bamboo pole across their shoulders on each end of which would be loads of ninety pounds, heaped in panniers. The panniers weighed five pounds each, and so the coolie would be carrying not less than one hundred and ninety pounds all day long. Life for them was hard, they worked until they died, and they died at quite a young age, worn out, human draught horses, treated worse than the beasts in the fields. And when they were worn out and fell dead sometimes they ended up in our dissecting rooms to continue the work of good, and this time by providing material for embryo doctors and surgeons who would acquire skill with which to treat living bodies.

We turned away from the edge of the cliff and faced into the very slight breeze which carried the sweet scent of the trees and the flowers. There was a slight grove of trees almost ahead, and we altered our steps slightly in order to go to them. A few yards from the cliff we stopped, aware of some strange sense of impending calamity, some sense of unease and tension, something inexplicable. We looked at each other questioningly, unable to decide what it was. Huang said, dubiously. "That cannot be thunder." "Of course not," I replied. "It is something very strange, something we know nothing about." We stood uncertainly, head on one side, listening. We looked about us, looked at the ground, at the trees, and then we looked at the clouds. It was from there that the noise was coming, a steady "brum-brum-brum" getting louder and louder, harsher and harsher. As we gazed upwards we saw, through a hole in the cloud base, a dark winged shape flit across. It was gone into the opposite cloud almost before we were aware of its presence. "My!" I shouted. "One of the Gods of the Sky

70

is come to take us off." There was nothing we could do. We just stood wondering what would happen next. The noise was thunderous, a noise of a sort that neither of us had heard before. Then, as we watched, a huge shape appeared, flinging wisps of clouds from it as if impatient of even the slight restraint of the clouds. It flashed out of the sky, skimmed straight over our heads, over the edge of the cliff with a sickening shriek, and with a buffet of tortured air. The noise ended and there was silence. We stood absolutely aghast, absolutely chilled, looking at each other. Then, upon a common impulse, we turned and ran toward the cliff edge to see what had happened to the thing from the sky, the thing which was so strange and so noisy. At the edge we flung ourselves prone and peered cautiously over at the sparkling river. There upon a sandy strip of ground was the strange, winged monster, now at rest. As we looked it coughed with a spurt of flame and a burst of black smoke. It made us jump and turn pale, but this was not the strangest thing. To our incredulous amazement and horror a piece opened in the side and two men got out. At that time I thought that was the most wonderful thing I had ever seen, but—we were wasting time up there. We sprang to our feet and raced for the path leading down. Down we sped through the street of steps, ignoring traffic, ignoring all courtesy, in our mad rush to get to the water's edge.

Down by the side of the river we could have stamped our feet with frustrated anger. There was not a boat to be had, not a boatman, no one. They had all flocked across the water to be where we wanted to be. But, yes! There was a boat behind a boulder. We turned towards it with the intention of launching it and going across, but as we reached it we saw an old, old man coming down a steep path carrying nets. "Hey, father," Huang shouted, "take us across." "Well," the old man said, "I don't want to go. What's it worth to you?" He tossed his nets in the boat and leaned against the side, old battered pipe in his mouth. He crossed his legs and looked as if he could have stayed there all night, just chatting. We were in a frenzy of impatience. "Come, on, old man, what's your charge?" The old man named a fantastic sum, a sum which would have bought his rotten old boat, we thought. But we were in a flurry of excitement, we would have given almost anything we had to get across to the other side. Huang bargained. I said, "Oh, don't let's waste time. Let's give him half what he asks." The old man jumped at it. It was about ten times more than he had expected. He jumped at it, so we rushed for his boat. "Steady on, young gentlemen, steady on. You'll wreck my boat," he said. "Oh, come on, grandpa," said Huang, "hurry up. The day is getting old." The old fellow leisurely got aboard, creaking with rheumatism, grunting. Slowly he picked up a pole, and poled us out into the stream. We were fidgeting, trying mentally to move the boat more rapidly, but nothing would hurry the old man. In the centre of the stream some eddy of current caught us and swung us around, then he got the boat on the right course again, and we went across to the far bank. To save time, as we were approaching, I counted out the money and pushed it at the old man. He was certainly quick to take it. Then, without waiting for the boat to touch, we jumped knee-deep in water, and ran up the bank.

Before us was that wonderful machine, that incredible machine, which had come from the sky, and which had brought men with it. We looked at it in awe, and were amazed at our own temerity in daring to approach like this. Other people were there, too, but they were staying a respectable distance away. We moved forward, we moved close to it, under it, feeling the rubber tyres on the wheels, punching them. We moved to the stern and saw that here there was no wheel, but a bar of springy metal with a thing like a shoe at the end. "Ah," I said, "that'll be a skid to slow it down as it lands. We had a thing like that on my

72

kites." Gingerly, half frightened, we fingered the side of the machine, we looked with incredulity as we found that it was a sort of fabric, painted in some way and stretched on a wooden frame. Now, this really was something! About half way between the wings and the tail we touched a panel, and we nearly fainted with shock as it opened, and a man dropped lightly to the ground. "Well," he said, "you certainly seem to be very interested." "We are indeed," I replied. "I've flown a thing like this, a silent one in Tibet." He looked at me and his eyes went wide. "Did you say in Tibet?" he asked. "I did," I answered. Huang broke in, "My friend is a living Buddha, a lama, studying in Chungking. He used to fly in man-lifting kites," he said. The man from the air machine looked interested. "That is fascinating," he said. "Will you come inside where we can sit down and talk?" He turned and led the way in. Well, I thought, I have had many experiences. If this man can trust himself inside the thing—so can I. So I entered as well, with Huang following my example. I had seen a thing larger than this in the Highlands of Tibet, in which the Gods of the Sky had flown straight out of the world. But that had been different, not so frightening, because the machine that they had used had been silent, but this had roared and torn at the air, and shook.

Inside there were seats, quite comfortable seats, too. We sat down. That man, he kept asking me questions about Tibet, questions which I thought absolutely stupid. Tibet was so commonplace, so ordinary, and here he was, in the most marvellous machine that ever had been, talking of Tibet. Eventually, after much time and with a great amount of trouble, we got some information out of him instead. This was a machine that they called an aeroplane, a device which had engines to throw it through the sky. It was the engines which made the noise, he said. This particular one was made by the Americans and it had been bought by a Chinese firm in Shanghai who had been thinking of starting an airline from Shanghai to Chungking. The three men that we had seen were the pilot, a navigator, and engineer, on a trial flight. The pilot—the man to whom we were talking—said, "We are to interest notabilities and to give them a chance of flying so that they may approve of our venture." We nodded, thinking how marvellous it was, and how we wished that we were notabilities and would have a chance of flying. He went on, "You from Tibet, you are indeed a notability. Would you like to try this machine with us?" I said, "My goodness me, I would, as quickly as you like!" He motioned to Huang, and asked him to step outside, saying that he couldn't go. "Oh, no," I said, "Oh, no. If one goes, the other goes." So Huang was allowed to stay (he did not thank me later!). The two men who had got out before moved toward the plane and there were a lot of hand signals. They did something to the front, then there was a loud "bam" and they did something more. Suddenly there was a shocking noise, and terrible vibration. We clung on, thinking that there had been some accident, and we were being shaken to pieces. "Hang on," said the man. We couldn't hang on more tightly, so it was quite superfluous of him. "We are going to take off," he said. There was a simply appalling racket, jolts, bumps, and thuds, worse than the first time I went up in a man-lifting kite. This was far worse because in addition to the jolts, there was noise, abominable noise. There was a final thud, which nearly drove my head between my shoulders, and then a sensation as if someone were pressing me hard beneath and at the back. I managed to raise my head and look out of the window at the side. We were in the air, we were climbing. We saw the river lengthening into a silver thread, the two rivers joining together to make one. We saw the sampans and the junks as little toys like little chips of wood floating. Then we looked at Chungking, at the streets, at the steep streets up which we had toiled so laboriously. From this height they looked level, but over the side of the

74

cliff the terraced fields still clung precariously at the appalling steep slope. We saw the peasants toiling away, oblivious to us. Suddenly there was a whiteness, complete and utter obscurity, even the engine noises seemed muffled. We were in the clouds. A few minutes with streamers of cloud rushing by the windows, and the light became stronger. We emerged into the pale blue of the sky, flooded with the golden sunlight. As we looked down it was like gazing down on a frozen sea of snow, scintillatingly white, dazzling, eye-hurting with the intensity of the glare. We climbed and climbed, and I became aware that the man in charge of the machine was talking to me. "This is higher than you have been before," he said, "much higher than you have been before." "Not at all," I replied, "because when I started in a man-lifting kite I was already seventeen thousand feet high." That surprised him. He turned to look out of the side window, the wing dipped, and we slid sideways in a screaming dive. Huang turned a pale green, a horrible colour, and unmentionable things happened to him. He lurched out of his seat, and lay face down on the bottom of the plane. He was not a pleasant sight, but nothing pleasant was happening to him. I—I was always immune to air-sickness, and I felt nothing at all except mild pleasure at the manoeuvres. Not Huang, he was frightfully upset by it. By the time we landed he was just a quivering mass who occasionally emitted a painful groan. Huang was not a good airman! Before we landed the man shut off his engines and we drifted in the sky, gradually getting lower, and lower. There was only the "swish" of the wind past our wings, and only the drumming of the fabric at the sides of the plane to tell us that we were in a man-made machine. Suddenly, as we were getting quite near the ground, the man switched on his engines again and we were once more deafened by the ear-shattering roar of many hundreds of horse-power. A circle, and we came in to land. A violent bump, and a screech from the tail skid, and we clattered to a stop. Again the engines were switched off and the pilot and I rose to get out. Poor Huang, he was not ready to rise. We had to carry him out and lay him on the sand to recover.

I am afraid that I was quite hard-hearted; Huang was lying face down in the yellow sand of the spit upon which we had landed in the middle of the mile-wide river. He was lying face down, making peculiar sounds and motions, and I was glad that he was not able to rise. Glad, because it gave me a good excuse to stop and talk with the man who had flown the machine. Talk we did. Unfortunately he wanted to talk about Tibet. What was the country like for flying? Could planes land there? Could an army land there dropped by parachute? Well, I hadn't the vaguest idea what parachutes were, but I said "No," to be on the safe side! We came to an arrangement. I told him about Tibet and he told me about aircraft. Then he said, "I would feel deeply honoured if you would meet some of my friends who also are interested in the Tibetan mysteries." Well, what did I want to meet his friends for? I was just a student at the college, and I wanted to become a student of the air, and all this fellow was thinking of was the social side of things. In Tibet I had been one of the very few who had flown. I had flown high above the mountains in a man-lifting kite, but although the sensation had been wonderful, and the silence soothing, yet the kite had still been tethered to the earth. It could merely go up in the air, it could not fly over the land, wherever the pilot wanted to fly. It was tethered like the yak at pasture. I wanted to know more of this roaring machine that flew as I had dreamed of flying, that could fly anywhere, to any part of the world, the pilot told me, and all he was bothering about was—talk about Tibet!

For a time it seemed to be a deadlock. We sat on the sand facing each other with poor Huang groaning away to the side, and not receiving any sympathy from us. Eventually we came to an arrangement. I agreed to meet his friends

76

and tell them a few things about Tibet and about the mysteries of Tibet. I agreed to give a few lectures about it. He, in his turn, would take me in the aeroplane again and explain how the thing worked. We walked around the machine first, he pointed out various things. The fins, the rudder, the elevators—all sorts of things. Then we got in and sat down, side by side, right in the front. In front of each of us now there was a kind of stick with half a wheel attached to it. The wheel could be rotated, left or right, while the whole stick could be pulled back or pushed forward. He explained to me how the pulling back would make a plane rise, and pushing forward would make it sink, and turning would also turn the machine. He pointed out the various knobs and switches. Then the engines were started and behind glass dials I saw quivering pointers which altered their position as the rates of the engines varied. We spent a long time, he did his part well, he explained everything. Then, with the engines stopped, we got out and he took off inspection covers and pointed out various details. Carburettors, sparking plugs, and many other things.

That evening I met his friends as promised. They were, of course, Chinese. They were all connected with the army. One of them told me that he knew Chiang Kai-Shek well, and, he said, the Generalissimo was trying to raise the nucleus of a technical army. Trying to raise the general standard of the services in the Chinese army. He said that in a few days' time one or two planes, smaller planes, would arrive at Chungking. They were planes, he told me, which had been purchased from the Americans. After that I had little thought in my head beyond flying. How could I get in one of these craft? How could I make it go up in the air? How could I learn to fly?

Huang and I were leaving the hospital a few days later when out of the heavy clouds stretching above our heads darted two silver shapes, two single-seater fighter planes which had come from Shanghai as promised. They circled over Chungking, and circled again. Then, as if they had just spotted exactly where to land, they dived down in close formation. We wasted no time. We hurried down the street of steps, and made our way across to the sand. There were two Chinese pilots standing beside their machines, busily engaged in polishing off marks of their flight through dirty clouds. Huang and I approached them, and made our presence known to the leader of the two, a Captain Po Ku. Huang had made it very clear to me that nothing would induce him to go up into the air again. He had thought that he would die after his first—and last—flight.

Captain Po Ku said, "Ah, yes, I have heard about you. I was actually wondering how to get in touch with you." And I was much flattered thereby. We talked for a time. He pointed out the differences between this machine and the passenger machine which we had seen before. This, as he pointed out, was a machine with a single seat, and one engine, but the other had been a three-engine type. We had little time to stay then, because we had to deal with our rounds, and it was with extreme reluctance that we left.

The next day we had half a day off and we made our way again, as early as possible, to the two planes. I asked the Captain when he was going to teach me to fly as promised. He said, "Oh, I could not possibly do that. I am just here by order of Chiang Kai-Shek. We are showing these planes." I kept on at him for that day, and when I saw him the day after he said, "You can sit in the machine, if you like. You will find that quite satisfying. Sit in and try the controls. This is how they work, look." And he stood on the wing root and pointed out the controls to me, showed me how they worked. They were much the same as those of the three-engine machine, but of course much simpler. That evening we took him and his companion— they left a guard of police on the machine—to the temple which was our home, and although I worked on them very hard I could not get any statement at all about when they

78

were going to teach me to fly. He said, "Oh, you may have to wait a long time. It takes months of training. It's impossible to fly a thing straight off as you want to. You would have to go to ground school, you would have to fly in a dual-seat machine, and you would have to do many hours before you were allowed in a plane such as ours."

The next day at the end of the afternoon we went down again. Huang and I crossed the river and landed on the sand. The two men were quite alone with their machine. The two machines were many yards apart. Apparently there was something wrong with that of Po Ku's friend, because he had got the engine cowling off, and tools were all over the place. Po Ku himself had the engine of his machine turning over. He was adjusting it. He stopped it, made an adjustment, and started it again. It went "phut-phut-phut" and did not run at all evenly. He was oblivious to us, as he stood on the wing, and fiddled about with the engine. Then, as the motor purred evenly, smoothly, like a well-pleased cat, he straightened up, wiping his hands on a piece of oily waste. He looked happy. He was turning to speak to us when his companion called urgently to him from the other plane. Po Ku went to stop the motor but the other pilot waved his hands frantically, so he just dropped to the ground from the wing and hurried off.

I looked at Huang. I said, "Ah ha, he said I could sit in, did he not? Well, I will sit in." "Lobsang," said Huang, "You are not thinking of anything rash are you?" "Not at all," I replied. "I could fly that thing, I know all about it." "But, man," said Huang, "you'll kill yourself." "Rubbish!" I said. "Haven't I flown kites? Haven't I been up in the air, and been free from air-sickness?" Poor Huang looked a bit crestfallen at that because his own airmanship was not at all good.

I looked toward the other plane, but the two pilots were far too busy to bother with me. They were kneeling on the sand doing something to part of an engine, obviously they

79

were quite engrossed. There was no one else about except Huang, so—I walked up to the plane. As I had seen the others do I kicked away the chocks in front of the wheels and hastily jumped in as the plane began to roll. The controls had been explained to me a few times and I knew which was the throttle, I knew what to do. I slammed it hard forward, hard against the stop, so hard that I nearly sprained my left wrist. The engine roared under full power as if it would tear itself free. Then we were off, absolutely speeding down that strip of yellow sand. I saw a flash where water and sand met. For a moment I felt panic, then I remembered: pull back. I pulled back on the control column hard, the nose rose, the wheels just kissed the waves and made spray, we were up. It felt as if an immense, powerful hand was pressing beneath me, pushing me up. The engine roared and I thought, "Must not let it go too fast, must throttle it back or it will fall to pieces." So I pulled the throttle control a quarter way back and the engine note became less. I looked over the side of the plane, and had quite a shock. A long way below were the white cliffs of Chungking. I was high, really high, so high that I could hardly pick out where I was. I was getting higher all the time. White cliffs, of Chungking? Where? Goodness! If I go any higher I shall fly out of the world, I thought. Just then there was a terrible shuddering, and I felt as if I was falling to pieces. The control in my hand was wrenched from my grasp. I was flung against the side of the machine which tilted, and lurched violently, and went spinning down to earth. For a moment I knew utter fright. I said to myself, "You've done it this time, Lobsang, my boy. You've been too clever for yourself. A few more seconds and they'll scrape you off the rock. Oh, why did I ever leave Tibet?" Then I reasoned out from what I had heard and from my kite flying experience. A spin; controls cannot operate, so I must give full throttle to try and get some directional control. No sooner had I thought of it than I pushed that throttle right forward again, and the engine roared anew. Then I grabbed the wildly threshing control and braced myself against the back of the seat. With my hands and my knees I forced that control forward. The nose dropped startlingly, as if the bottom had fallen out of the world. I had no safety belt and if I had not been clinging on very tightly to the controls I would have been shot out. It felt as if there were ice in my veins, as if someone was pushing snow down my back. My knees became strangely weak, the engine roared, the whine getting higher and higher. I was bald, but I am sure that had I not been the hair would have stood absolutely on end in spite of the air-stream. "Ouch, fast enough," I said to myself, and gently, oh, so gently, in case it broke off, I eased back that control. Gradually, terrifying slowly, the nose came up, and up, but in my excitement I forgot to level off. Up went the nose until the strange feeling made me look down, or was it up? I found the whole earth was above my head! For a moment I was completely at a loss to know what had happened. Then the plane gave a lurch and turned over into a dive again, so that the earth, the hard world beneath, was directly in front of the propeller. I had turned a somersault. I had flown upside down, braced on hands and knees in the cockpit, hanging upside down with no safety belt, and definitely without much hope. I admit I was frightened but I thought, "Well, if I can stay on the back of a horse, I can stay in a machine." So I let the nose drop some more and then gradually pulled back the stick. Again I felt as if a mighty hand was pushing me; this time, though, I pulled back the stick slowly, carefully, watching the ground all the time, and I was able to level off the plane in even flight. For a moment or two I just sat there, mopping the perspiration from my brow, thinking what a terrible affair it had been; first going straight down, then going straight up, then flying upside down, and now I did not know where I was.

I looked over the side, I peered at the ground, I turned

round and round, and I hadn't got the vaguest idea where I was. I might have been in the Gobi Desert. At last, when I had just about given up hope, inspiration struck me—just about everything in the cockpit had as well!—the river, where was it? Obviously, I thought, if I can find the river then I either go left or right, eventually I will go somewhere. So I turned the plane in a gentle circle, peering into the distance. At last I saw a faint silver thread on the horizon. I turned the plane in that direction, and kept it there. I pushed forward the throttle to get there more quickly, and then I pulled the throttle back again in case something broke off with all the noise I was making. I wasn't feeling too happy at this time. I had found that I was doing everything in extremes. I had pushed forward the throttle, the nose would rise with alarming rapidity, or I would pull back the throttle and the nose would fall with even more alarming suddenness. So now I was trying everything gently; it was a new attitude which I had adopted for the occasion.

When I was right over it, I turned again, and flew along that river, seeking the cliffs of Chungking. It was most bewildering. I could not find the place. Then I decided to come lower. Lower I circled, and circled, peering over the side looking for those white cliffs with the gashes which were the steep steps, looking for the terraced fields. They were hard to find. At last it dawned upon me that all those little specks on the river were the ships about Chungking. A little paddle steamer, the sampans, and the junks. So I went lower still. Then I saw a mere sliver of sand. Down I went, spiralling down like a hawk spiralling down in search of prey. The sandy spit became larger, and larger. Three men were looking up, petrified with horror, three men, Po Ku and his fellow pilot and Huang, feeling quite certain, as they later told me, that they had lost a plane. But now I was fairly confident, too confident. I had got up in the air, I had flown upside down, I had found Chungking. Now, I thought,

I am the world's best pilot. Just then I had an itch in my left leg where there was a bad scar from the time when I was burned in the lamasery. Unconsciously I suppose I twitched my leg; the plane rocked, a tornado of wind struck my left cheek, the nose went down as the wing tilted, and soon I was in a screaming sideslip. Once again I pushed forward the throttle and gingerly pulled back on the control column. The plane shuddered and the wings vibrated. I thought they were going to fall off! By a miracle they held. The plane bucked like an angry horse, and then slid into level flight. My heart was fairly pounding at the effort and with the fright. I flew again in a circle over the little patch of sand. "Well, now," I thought to myself, "I've got to land the thing. How am I going to do that?" The river here was a mile wide. To me it looked as if it was inches and the little patch on which I had to land was diminutive. I circled wondering what to do. Then I remembered what they had told me, how they had explained flying. So I looked for some smoke to see which way the wind was blowing, because they had told me I had to land into wind. It was blowing up-river, I saw by a bonfire which had been lit on the bank of the river. I turned and flew up-stream, up many miles, and then I reversed my course, so that I was facing down-river and into wind. As I flew towards Chungking I gradually eased back the throttle so that I was going slower and slower, and so that the plane would sink and sink. Once I eased it back too much, and the machine stalled and rocked, and dropped like a stone, leaving my heart and stomach, or so it felt, hanging on a cloud. Very quickly indeed I pushed forward the throttle and pulled back the control column, but I had to turn round again and make my way up-river once more, and start all over again. I was getting tired of this flying business, and wishing that I had never started it at all. It was one thing, I thought, to get it up in the air, but a very different thing to get down —in one piece.

The roaring of the engine was becoming monotonous. I was thankful to see Chungking coming in sight again. I was low now, going slowly, just above the river, between huge rocks which often looked white, but now, through the oblique rays of the sun, looked a greenish black. As I approached the sandy spit in the middle of the too narrow river—I could have done with several miles of width!—I saw three figures hopping up and down with excitement. I was so interested watching them that I just forgot all about landing. By the time it had occurred to me that this was the place I had to alight, it had passed beneath my wheels, beneath the tail skid. So, with a sigh of weary resignation, I pushed that hated throttle forward to gain speed. I pulled back on the control to gain height, and went over in a sharp left swing. Now I was facing up-river again, sick of the scenery, sick of Chungking, sick of everything.

I turned once more down-river, and into wind. Across to the right I saw a beautiful sight. The sun was going down, and it was red, red and huge. Going down. It reminded me that I had to go down too, and I thought I would go down and crash and die, and I felt to myself that I was not yet ready to join the Gods, there was so much to be done. This reminded me of the Prophecy, and I knew that I had nothing more to worry about. The Prophecy! Of course I would land safely and all would be well.

Thinking of that almost made me forget Chungking. Here it was nearly beneath the left wing. I gently eased on the rudder-bar to make sure that the sandy spit of yellow sand was dead in front of the engine. I slowed down more, and more. The plane gradually sank. I pulled back the throttle so that I was about ten feet above the water as the engine note died. To be sure that there was no fire if I crashed I switched off the engine. Then, very, very gently, I pushed forward the control column to lose more height. Straight in front of the engine I saw sand and water as if I was aiming directly at it. So gently I pulled back the control column.

There was a tug, and a jar, then a bounce. Once again a scraping noise, a tug, and a jar, and then a rumbling creak as if everything was falling to pieces. I was on the ground. The plane had just about landed itself. For a moment I sat quite still, hardly believing that it was all over, that the noise of the engine was not really there, but that it was just imagination in my ears. Then I looked around. Po Ku and his companion and Huang came racing up, red in the face with the effort, breathless. They skidded to a stop just beneath me. Po Ku looked at me, looked at the plane, looked at me again. Then he went really pale-faced with shock and utter relief. He was so relieved that he was quite unable to be angry. After a long, long interval Po Ku said, "That settles it. You will have to join the Force or I shall get into very serious trouble." "All right," I said, "suits me fine. There's nothing in this flying business. But I would like to learn the approved method!" Po Ku turned red in the face again, and then laughed. "You're a born pilot, Lobsang Rampa," he said. "You'll get your chance to learn to fly." So that was the first step toward leaving Chungking. As a surgeon and as a pilot my services would be of use elsewhere.

Later in the day, when we were talking over the whole matter, I asked Po Ku why, if he had been so worried, he had not come up in the other plane to show me the way back. He said, "I wanted to, but you had flown off with the starter and all, so I could not."

Huang, of course, spread the story, as did Po Ku and his companion, and for several days I was the talk of the college and of the hospital, much to my disgust. Dr. Lee sent for me officially to administer a severe reprimand, but unofficially to congratulate me. He said that he would have liked to have done a thing like that himself in his younger days, but "There were no aircraft in my young days, Rampa. We had to go by horse or by foot." He said that now it fell to the lot of a wild Tibetan to give him the best

85

thrill that he had had for years. He added, "Rampa, what did their auras look like as you flew over them and they thought that you were going to crash on them?" He had to laugh as I said that they looked completely terrified and their auras had contracted to a pale blue blot, shot through with maroon red streaks. I said, "I am glad there was no one there to see what my aura was like. It must have been terrible. Certainly it felt so."

Not so long after this I was approached by a representative of Generalissimo Chiang Kai-Shek and offered the opportunity to learn to fly properly and be commissioned in the Chinese Forces. The officer who came to me said, "If we have time before the Japanese invade seriously, we would like to establish a special corps so that those people who are injured and cannot be moved can receive help from men of the air who are also surgeons." So it came about that I had other things to study beside human bodies. I had to study oil circulation as well as the circulation of the blood. I had to study the framework of aircraft as well as the skeletons of humans. They were of equal interest and they had many points in common.

So the years went on, and I became a qualified doctor and a qualified pilot, trained in both, working in a hospital and flying in my spare time. Huang dropped out of it. He was not interested in flying and the mere thought of a plane made him turn pale. Po Ku, instead, stayed with me because it had been seen how well we got on together and we made indeed a satisfactory team.

Flying was a wonderful sensation. It was glorious to be high up in an aeroplane, and to switch off the engine and to glide and to soar in the way that the birds did. It was so much like astral travelling which I do and which anyone else can do provided their heart is reasonably healthy and they will have the patience to persevere.

Do YOU know what astral travelling is? Can YOU recall the pleasures of soaring, of drifting over the house tops, going across the oceans, perhaps, to some far distant land? We can all do it. It is merely when the more spiritual part of the body casts aside its physical covering, and soars into other dimensions and visits other parts of the world at the end of its "silver cord." There is nothing magical about it, nothing wrong. It is natural and wholesome, and in days gone by all men could travel astrally without let or hindrance. The Adepts of Tibet and many of India travel in their astral from place to place, and there is nothing strange in it. In religious books the world over, the Bibles of all religions, there is mention of such things as "the silver cord" and the "golden bowl." This so-called silver cord is merely a shaft of energy, radiant energy, which is capable of infinite extension. It is not a material cord like a muscle, or artery, or piece of string, but it is life itself, is the energy which connects the physical body and the astral body.

Man has many bodies. For the moment we are interested only in the physical and in the next stage, the astral. We may think that when we are in a different state we can walk through walls, or fall through floors. We can, but we can only walk or fall through floors of a different density. In the astral stage things of this everyday world are no barrier to our passage. Doors of a house would not keep one in or keep one out. But in the astral world there are also doors and walls which to us in the astral are as solid, as containing, as the doors and walls of this earth are to the physical body.

Have YOU seen a ghost? If so it was probably an astral entity, perhaps an astral projection of someone you know, or someone visiting you from another part of the world. You may, at some time, have had a particularly vivid dream. You may have dreamed that you were floating like a balloon, up into the sky, held by a string, a cord. You may have been able to look down from the sky, from the other end of this cord, and have found that your body was rigid,

87

pallid, immovable. If you kept calm at that disconcerting sight you may have found yourself floating, floating off, drifting like a piece of thistledown on a breeze. A little later you may have found yourself in some distant land, or some remote district known to you. If you thought anything about it in the morning you would probably put it down as a dream. It was astral travelling.

Try this: when you go to sleep at night think vividly that you are going to visit someone you know well. Think of how you are going to visit that person. It may be some-one in the same town. Well, as you are lying down keep quite still, relaxed, at ease. Shut your eyes and imagine yourself floating off the bed, out through the window, and floating over the street—knowing that nothing can hurt you —knowing that you cannot fall. In your imagination follow the exact line that you will take, street by street, until you get to the house that you want. Then imagine how you are going to enter the house. Doors do not bother you now, remember, nor do you have to knock. You will be able to see your friend, the person whom you have come to visit. That is, you will be able to if your motives are pure. There is no difficulty at all, nothing dangerous, nothing harmful. There is only one law: your motives must be pure.

Here it is again, repetition if you like, but it is much better to approach it from one or two view-points so that you can see how utterly simple this is. As you lie upon your bed, alone with no one to disturb you, with your bedroom door locked so that no one can come in, keep calm. Imagine that you are gently disengaging from your body. There is no harm, nothing can hurt you. Imagine that you hear various little creaks and that there are numerous jolts, small jolts, as your spiritual force leaves the physical and solidifies above.

Imagine that you are forming a body the exact counter-part of your physical body, and that it is floating above the physical, weightlessly. You will experience a slight swaying, a minute rise and fall. There is nothing to be afraid of, there is nothing to worry about. This is natural, harmless. As you keep calm you will find that gradually your now-freed spirit will drift until you float a few feet off. Then you can look down at yourself, at your physical body. You will see that your physical and your astral bodies are connected by a shining silver cord, a bluish silver cord, which pulsates with life, with the thoughts that go from physical to astral, and from astral to physical. Nothing can hurt you so long as your thoughts are pure.

Nearly everyone has had an experience of astral travelling. Cast your mind back and think if you can remember this: have you ever been asleep and had the impression that you were swaying, falling, falling, and then you awoke with a jolt just before you crashed into the ground? That was astral travelling done the wrong way, the unpleasant way. There is no need for you to suffer that inconvenience or unpleasantness. It was caused by the difference in vibration between the physical and the astral bodies. It may have been that when you were floating down to enter the physical body after making a journey, some noise, some draught, or some interruption, caused a slight discrepancy in position and the astral body came down to the physical body not exactly in the right position, so there was a jolt, a jar. You can liken it to stepping off a moving bus. The bus, which is, let us say, the astral body, is doing ten miles an hour. The ground, which we will call the physical body, does not move. In the short space between leaving the bus platform and hitting the ground you have to slow down or experience a jerk. So, if you have had this falling sensation, then you have had astral travelling even if you did not know it, because the jerk of coming back to what one would call a "bad landing" would erase the memory of what you did, of what you saw. In any event, without training you would have been asleep when you were astral travelling. So you would have merely thought that you had dreamed,

89

"I dreamed last night that I visited such-and-such a place, and saw so-and-so." How many times have you said that? All a dream! But was it? With a little practice you can do astral travelling when you are fully awake and you can retain the memory of what you saw, and what you did. The big disadvantage of course with astral travelling is just this: when you travel in the astral you can take nothing with you, nor can you take anything back, so it is a waste of time to think that you will go somewhere by astral travelling, because you cannot even take money, not even a handkerchief, but only your spirit.

People with bad hearts should not practise astral travelling. For them it could be dangerous. But there is no danger whatever for those with sound hearts, because so long as your motives are pure, so long as you do not contemplate evil or gain over another, no harm whatever can happen.

Do you want to travel astrally? This is the easiest way to set about it. First of all remember this: it is the first law of psychology, and it stipulates that in any battle between the will and the imagination, the imagination *always* wins. So always imagine that you can do a thing, and if you imagine it strongly enough you can do it. You can do anything. Here is an example to make it clear.

Anything that you really imagine you can do, that you can do, no matter how difficult or impossible it is to the onlooker. Anything which your imagination tells you is impossible, then, to you, it is impossible, no matter how much your will tries to force you on. Think of it in this way; there are two houses thirty-five feet high, and ten feet apart. A plank is stretched between them at roof level. The plank is, perhaps, two feet wide. If you want to walk across that plank your imagination would cause you to picture all the hazards, the wind causing you to sway, or perhaps something in the wood causing you to stumble. You might, your imagination says, become giddy, but no matter the cause, your imagination tells you that the journey would be impossible for you, you would fall and be killed. Well, no matter how hard you try, if you once imagine that you cannot do it, then do it you cannot, and that simple little walk across the plank would be an impossible journey for you. No amount of will power at all would enable you to cross safely. Yet, if that plank was on the ground you could walk its length without the slightest hesitation. Which wins in a case like this? Will power? Or imagination? Again, if you imagine that you can walk the plank between the two houses, then you can do it easily, it does not matter at all if the wind is blowing or even if the plank shakes, so long as you imagine that you can cross safely. People walk tight ropes, perhaps they even cross on a cycle, but no will power would make them do it. It is just imagination.

It is an unfortunate thing that we have to call this "imagination," because, particularly in the west, that indicates something fanciful, something unbelievable, and yet imagination is the strongest force on earth. Imagination can make a person think he is in love, and love thus becomes the second strongest force. We should call it controlled imagination. Whatever we call it we must always remember: in any battle between the will and the imagination, the imagination ALWAYS WINS. In the east we do not bother about will power, because will power is a snare, a trap, which chains men to earth. We rely on controlled imagination, and we get results.

If you have to go to the dentist for an extraction, you imagine the horrors that await you there, the absolute agony, you imagine every step of the extraction. Perhaps the insertion of the needle, and the jerking as the anaesthetic is pumped in, and then the probing about of the dentist. You imagine yourself fainting, or screaming, or bleeding to death, or something. All nonsense, of course, but very, very real to you, and when you get into the chair you suffer a lot of pain which is quite unnecessary. This is an example of imagination wrongly use. That is not controlled imagination, it is imagination run wild, and no one should permit that.

Women will have been told shocking tales about the pains, the dangers, of having children. At the time of the birth the mother-to-be, thinking of all these pains to come, tenses herself, makes herself rigid, so that she gets a twinge of pain. That convinces her that what she imagined is perfectly true, that having a baby is a very painful affair, so she tenses some more, and gets another pain, and in the end she has a perfectly horrible time. Not so in the east. People imagine that having a baby is easy, and painless, and so it is. Women in the east have their babies, and perhaps go on with their housework a few hours after, because they know how to control imagination.

You have heard of "brain-washing" as practised by the Japanese, and by the Russians? That is a process of preying upon one's imagination, and of causing one to imagine things which the captor wants one to imagine. This is the captor's method of controlling the prisoner's imagination, so that the prisoner will admit anything at all, even if such admission costs the prisoner's life. Controlled imagination avoids all this because the victim who is being brain-washed, or even tortured, can imagine something else, and then the ordeal is perhaps not so great, certainly the victim does not succumb to it.

Do you know the process of feeling a pain? Let us stick a pin into a finger. Well, we put the point of the pin against the flesh, and we wait with acute apprehension the moment when the point of the pin will penetrate the skin, and a spurt of blood will follow. We concentrate all our energies on examining the spot. If we had a pain in our foot we would forget all about it in the process of sticking a pin in a finger. We concentrate the whole of our imagination upon that finger, upon the point of that pin. We imagine the pain it will cause to the exclusion of all else. Not so the Easterner, who has been trained. He does not dwell upon the finger, or the perforation to follow, he dissipates his imagination —controlled imagination—all over the body, so that the pain which is actually caused to the finger is spread out over the whole of the body, and so in such a small thing as a pin-prick it is not felt at all. That is controlled imagination. I have seen people with a bayonet stuck in them. They have not fainted, or screamed, because they knew the bayonet thrust was coming, and they imagined something else—controlled imagination again—and the pain was spread throughout the whole body area, instead of being localised, so the victim was able to survive the pain of the bayonet thrust.

Hypnotism is another good example of imagination. In this the person who is being hypnotised surrenders his imagination to the person who is hypnotising. The person being hypnotised imagines that he is succumbing to the influence of the other. He imagines that he is becoming drowsy, that he is falling under the influence of the hypnotist. So, if the hypnotist is sufficiently persuasive, and convinces the imagination of the patient, the patient succumbs, and becomes pliable to the commands of the hypnotist, and that is all there is to it. In the same way, if a person goes in for auto-hypnosis, he merely imagines that he is falling under the influence of—HIMSELF! And so he does become controlled by his Greater Self. This imagination, of course, is the basis of faith cures; people build up, and build up, and imagine that if they visit such-and-such a place, or are treated by such-and-such a person, they will get cured on the instant. Their imagination, in such a case, really does issue commands to the body, and so a cure is effected, and that cure is permanent so long as the imagination retains command, so long as no doubt of the imagination creeps in.

Just one more homely little example, because this matter of controlled imagination is the most important thing that you can ever understand. Controlled imagination can mean difference between success and failure, health and illness. But here it is; have you ever been riding a cycle on an absolutely straight, open road, and then ahead of you seen a big stone, perhaps a few feet from your front wheel? You might have thought, "Oh, I can't avoid that!" And sure enough you could not. Your front wheel would wobble, and no matter how you tried you would quite definitely run into that stone just like a piece of iron being drawn to a magnet. No amount of will power at all would enable you to avoid that stone. Yet if you imagined that you could avoid it, then avoid it you would. No amount of will power enables you to avoid that stone. Remember that most important rule, because it can mean all the difference in the world to you. If you go on willing yourself to do a thing when the imagination opposes it, you will cause a nervous breakdown. That actually is the cause of many of these mental illnesses. Present-day conditions are quite difficult, and a person tries to subdue his imagination (instead of controlling it) by the exercise of will power. There is an inner conflict, inside the mind, and eventually a nervous breakdown occurs. The person can become neurotic, or even insane. The mental homes are absolutely filled with patients who have willed themselves to do a thing when their imagination thought otherwise. And yet, it is a very simple matter indeed to control the imagination, and to make it work for one. It is imagination—controlled imagination—which enables a man to climb a high mountain, or to fly a very fast plane and break a record, or do any of those feats which we read about. Controlled imagination. The person imagines that he can do this, or can do that, and so he can. He has the imagination telling him that he can, and he has the will "willing" him to do it. That means complete success. So, if you want to make your path an easy one, and your life pleasant in the same way as the Easterner does, forget about will power, it is just a snare, and a delusion. Remember only controlled imagination. What you imagine, that you can do. Imagination, faith, are they not one?

CHAPTER FIVE

The Other Side of Death

OLD Tsong-tai was dead, curled up as if he were asleep. We were all sick at heart. The ward was hushed with sympathy. We knew death, we were facing death and suffering all day long, sometimes all night long too. But old Tsong-tai was dead.

I looked down at his lined brown face, at the skin drawn tight like parchment over a framework, like the string drawn tight on a kite as it hummed in the wind. Old Tsong-tai was a gallant old gentleman. I looked down at this thin face, his noble head, and the sparse white hairs of his beard. Years before he had been a high-ranking official at the Palace of the Emperors in Peking. Then had come the revolution and the old man had been driven away in the terrible aftermath of war and of civil war. He had made his way to Chungking, and had set up as a market gardener, starting again from the bottom, scratching a bare existence from the hard soil. He had been an educated old man, one to whom it was a delight to talk. Now his voice was stilled for ever. We had worked hard to save him.

The hard life which he had had, had proved too much for him. One day he had been working in his field, and he had dropped. For hours he had lain there, too ill to move, too ill to call for assistance. They had come for us eventually, when it was too late. We had taken the old man to the hospital and I had tended him, my friend. Now there was nothing more that I could do except see that he had

95

burial of the type that he would want to have, and to see too that his aged wife was freed from want.

I lovingly closed his eyes, the eyes that would no longer gaze at me quizzically as I plied him with questions. I made sure that the bandage was tight around his jaws so that his mouth would not sag, the mouth that had given me so much encouragement, so much teaching in Chinese and Chinese history, for it had been my wont to call upon the old man of an evening, to take him little things, and to talk with him as one man to another. I drew the sheet over him and straightened up. The day was far advanced. It was long past the hour at which I should have left, for I had been on duty for more than seventeen hours, trying to help, trying to cure.

I made my way up the hill, past the shops so brightly lighted, for it was dark. I went on past the last of the houses. The sky was cloudy. Below in the harbour the water had been lashing up at the quay side and the ships were rocking and tossing at their moorings.

The wind moaned and sighed through the pine trees as I walked along the road toward the lamasery. For some reason I shivered. I was oppressed with a horrid dread. I could not get the thought of death out of my mind. Why should people have to die so painfully? The clouds overhead scurried swiftly by like people intent on their business, obscuring the face of the moon, blowing clear, allowing shafts of moonlight to illuminate the dark fir trees. Then the clouds would come together again, and the light would be shut off, and all would be gloomy, and dark, and foreboding. I shivered.

As I walked along the road my footsteps echoed hollowly in the silence, echoed as if someone were following me close behind. I was ill at ease, again I shivered and drew my robe more tightly around me. "Must be sickening for something," I said to myself. "I really feel most peculiar. Can't think what it can be." Just then I came to the entrance of the little path through the trees, the little path which led up the hill to the lamasery. I turned right, away from the main road. For some moments I walked along until I came to a little clearing at the side of the path where a fallen tree had brought others crashing down. Now, one was flat upon the ground and the others lay at crazy angles. "I think I'll sit down for a moment. Don't know what's happened to me." I said to myself. With that I turned into the clearing and looked for a clean place upon the trunk of a tree. I sat down and tucked my robes around my legs to protect me from the chill wind. It was eerie. All the small sounds of the night broke in upon me, queer shudders, squeaks, and rustles. Just then scurrying clouds overhead parted, and a brilliant beam of moonlight flooded into the clearing, illuminating all as if in the clearest day. It seemed strange to me, light, moonlight as bright as that, as bright as the brightest sunlight. I shivered, then jumped to my feet in alarm: A man was approaching through the trees at the other side of the clearing. I stared in utter incredulity. It was a Tibetan lama. A lama was coming toward me with blood pouring from his chest, staining his robes, his hands too were covered with blood, dripping red. He walked toward me, and I reeled back and almost tripped over the bole of a tree. I sank down and sat in terror. "Lobsang, Lobsang, are you afraid of ME?" a well-known voice exclaimed. I stood up, rubbed my eyes, and then rushed toward that figure. "Stop!" he said. "You cannot touch me. I have come to say goodbye to you, for this day I have finished my span upon the earth, and I am about to depart. Shall we sit and talk?" I turned, dumbly, heart-broken, stunned, and resumed my seat upon the fallen tree. Overhead the clouds whirled by, the leaves of the trees rustled, a night bird flitted overhead intent only upon food, upon prey, oblivious to us, and our business. Somewhere at the end of the trunk upon which we sat some small creature of the night rustled and squeaked as it turned over rotting vegetation in search of food. Here in this desolate clearing, wind-swept, and bleak, I sat and talked with a ghost, the ghost of my Guide, the Lama Mingyar Dondup, who had returned from beyond Life to talk to me.

He sat beside me as he had sat beside me so many times before away in Lhasa. He sat not touching me, perhaps three yards' distance from me. "Before you left Lhasa, Lobsang, you asked me to tell you when my span upon earth had finished. My span has now finished. Here I am." I looked at him, the man I knew above all others. I looked at him and I could hardly believe—even with all my experience of such things—that this man was no longer of the flesh, but a spirit, that his silver cord had been severed, and the golden bowl shattered. He looked to me to be solid, entire, as I had known him. He was dressed in his robes, in his brick red cassock with the golden cloak. He looked tired as if he had travelled far and painfully. I could see well that for a long time past he had neglected his own welfare in the service of others. "How wan he looks," I thought. Then he partly turned, in a habit that I so well remembered, and as he did so I saw a dagger in his back. He shrugged slightly and settled himself, and faced me. I froze with horror as I saw that the point of the dagger was protruding from his chest, and the blood had poured from the wound, had run down and saturated the golden robe. Before it had been as a blur to me, I had not taken in the details, I had just seen a lama with blood on his chest, blood on his hands, but now I was gazing more closely. The hands I saw were blood-stained where he had clutched himself as the dagger came through his chest. I shivered, and my blood ran cold within me. He saw my gaze, he saw the horror in my face, and he said, "I came like this deliberately, Lobsang, so that you could see what happened. Now that you have seen me thus, see me as I am." The blood-stained form vanished in a flash, a flash of golden light, and then it was replaced by a vision of surpassing beauty and purity. It was a Being who had advanced

98

far upon the path of evolution. One who had attained Buddhahood.

Then as clear as the sound of a temple bell, his voice came to me, not perhaps to my physical ears but to my inner consciousness. A voice of beauty, resonant, full of power, full of life, Greater Life. "My time is short, Lobsang, I must soon be on my way, for there are those who await me. But you, my friend, my companion in so many adventures, I had to visit you first, to cheer you, to reassure you, and to say 'Farewell' for a time. Lobsang, we have talked so long together in the past on these matters. Again I say to you, your way will be hard, and dangerous, and long, but you will succeed in spite of all, in spite of the opposition and the jealousy of the men of the West."

For a long time we talked, talked of things too intimate to discuss. I was warm and comfortable, the clearing was filled with a golden glow, brighter than the brightest sunlight, and the warmth was the warmth of a summer noon. I was filled with true Love. Then, suddenly, my Guide, my beloved Lama Mingyar Dondup, rose to his feet, but his feet were not in contact with the earth. He stretched out his hands above my head and gave me his blessing, and he said, "I shall be watching over you, Lobsang, to help you as much as I can, but the way is hard, the blows will be many and even before this day has ended you will receive yet another blow. Bear up, Lobsang, bear up as you have borne up in the past. My blessing be upon you." I raised my eyes, and before my gaze he faded and was gone, the golden light died and was no more, and the shadows of the night rushed in and the wind was cold. Overhead the clouds raced by in angry turmoil. Small creatures of the night chattered and rustled. There was a squeak of terror from some victim of a larger creature as it breathed its last.

For a moment I stood as if stunned. Then I flung myself to the ground beside the tree trunk, and clawed at the moss, and for a time I was not a man in spite of all my training, in spite of all I knew. Then I seemed to hear within me that dear voice once again. "Be of good cheer, my Lobsang, be of good cheer for this is not the end, for all that for which we strive is worthwhile and shall be. This is not the end." So I rose shakily to my feet, and I composed my thoughts, and I brushed off my robe, and wiped my hands from the mud on the ground.

Slowly I continued my journey up the path, up the hill, to the lamasery. "Death," I thought, "I have been to the other side of death myself, but I returned. My Guide has gone beyond recall, beyond my reach. Gone, and I am alone, alone." So, with such thoughts in my mind I reached the lamasery. At the entrance were a number of monks who had just returned by other paths. Blindly I brushed by them, and made my way along into the darkness of the temple where the sacred images gazed at me and seemed to have understanding and compassion on their carven faces. I looked upon the Tablets of the Ancestors, the red banners with the golden ideographs, upon the ever-burning incense with its fragrant swirl of smoke hanging like a somnolent cloud between the floor and the high ceiling far overhead. I made my way to a distant corner, to a truly sacred spot, and I heard again, "Be of good cheer, Lobsang, be of good cheer, for this is not the end and that for which we strive is worthwhile and shall be. Be of good cheer." I sank down in the lotus position, and I dwelt upon the past and upon the present. How long I stayed thus I do not know. My world was toppling around me. Hardships were pressing upon me. My beloved Guide had gone from this world, but he had told me, "This is not the end, it is all worthwhile." Around me monks went about their business, dusting, preparing, lighting fresh incense, chanting, but none came to disturb my grief as I sat alone.

The night wore on. Monks made preparation for a service. The Chinese monks in their black robes, with their shaven heads with the incense marks burned into their skulls, looked like ghosts in the light of the flickering butter lamps. The priest of the temple in his five-faced Buddha crown came chanting by as the temple bugles were sounded and the silver bells were rung. I slowly rose to my feet and made my reluctant way to the Abbot. With him I discussed what had happened, and asked to be excused from the midnight service, saying that I was too sick at heart, too unwilling to show my grief to the world of the lamasery. He said, "No, my brother. You have cause to rejoice. You have passed beyond death and returned, and this day you have heard from your Guide, and you have seen the living proof of his Buddhahood. My brother you should not feel sorrow for the parting is but temporary. Take the midnight service, my brother, and rejoice that you have seen that which is denied to so many."

"Training is all very well," I thought. "I know as well as any that death on earth is birth into the Greater life. I know that there is no death, that this is but the World of Illusion, and that the real life is yet to come, when we leave this nightmare stage, this earth, which is but a school to which we come to learn our lessons. Death? There is no such thing. Why then am I so disheartened?" The answer came to me almost before I asked myself the question. I am despondent because I am selfish, because I have lost that which I love, because that which I love is now beyond my reach. I am selfish indeed, for he who has gone has gone to glorious life, while I am still ensnared in the toils of the earth, left to suffer on, to strive on, to do that task for which I came in the same way as a student at a school has to strive on until he has passed his final examinations. Then with new qualifications he can set forth unto the world to learn all over again. I am selfish, I said, for I would keep my beloved Guide here upon this terrible earth for my own selfish gain.

Death? There is nothing to be afraid of in death. It is

life of which we should be afraid, life which enables us to make so many mistakes.

There is no need to fear death. There is no need to fear the passing from this life to the Greater Life. There is no need to fear hell, for there is no such place, there is no such thing as a Day of Judgment. Man judges himself, and there is no sterner judge than man of his own infirmities, his own weakness, when he passes beyond life on earth and when the scales of false values drop from his eyes and when he can see Truth. So all you who fear death know this from one who has been beyond death, and has returned. There is naught to fear. There is no Day of Judgment except that which you make yourself. There is no hell. Everyone, no matter who they are, nor what they have done, is given a chance. No one is ever destroyed. No one is ever too bad to be given another chance. We fear the death of others because it deprives us of their well loved company, because we are selfish, and we fear our own death because it is a journey into the Unknown, and that which we do not understand, that which we do not know, that we fear. But—there is no death, there is only birth into a Greater Life. In the early days of all religions that was the teaching; there is no death, there is only birth into the Greater Life. Through generation after generation of priests the true teaching has been altered, corrupted, until they threaten with fear, with brimstone and sulphur, and tales of hell. They do all this to boost up their own power, to say, "We are the priests, we have the keys of heaven. Obey us or you will go to hell." But I have been to the other side of death and have returned, as have many lamas. We know the truth. We know that always there is hope. No matter what one has done, no matter how guilty one may feel, one must strive on for there is always hope.

The Abbot of the lamasery had told me, "Take the midnight service, my brother, and tell of that which you have seen this day." I dreaded it. It was indeed an ordeal for me.

I felt sick at heart. The terrible oppression sat upon me, and I returned to a secluded corner of the temple to my meditation. So that terrible evening wore on, with the minutes feeling like hours, with the hours like days, and I thought I should never live through it. The monks came and went. There was activity around me in the body of the temple, but I was alone with my thoughts, thinking of the past, dreading the future.

But it was not to be. I was not to take the midnight service after all. As my Guide, the Lama Mingyar Dondup had warned me earlier in the evening another blow was yet to fall before the day was ended, a terrible blow. I was meditating in my quiet corner, thinking of the past and of the future. At about 11 o'clock of that night when all was quiet around me, I saw a figure approaching. It was an old, old lama, one of the *élite* of the temple of Lhasa, an old living Buddha who had not much longer to live on this earth. He approached from the deeper shadows where the flickering butter lamps did not penetrate. He approached, and about him was a bluish glow. Around his head the glow was yellow. He approached me with his hands outstretched, palm up, and said, "My son, my son, I have grave tidings for you. The Inmost One, the 13th Dalai Lama, the last of his line, is shortly to pass from this world." The old man, the lama who visited me, told me that the end of a cycle was approaching, and that the Dalai Lama was to leave. He told me that I should make full haste and return to Lhasa so that I could see him before it was too late. He told me that, then he said, "You must make all haste. Use whatever means you can to return. It is imperative that you leave this night." He looked at me, and I rose to my feet. As I did so he faded, he merged back into the shadows and was no more. His spirit had returned to his body which even then was at the Jo Kang in Lhasa.

Events were happening too quickly for me. Tragedy after tragedy, event after event. I felt dazed. My training had

103

been a hard one indeed. I had been taught about life and about death, and about showing no emotion, yet what can one do when one's beloved friends are dying in quick succession? Is one to remain stony hearted, frozen faced, and aloof, or is one to have warm feelings? I loved these men. Old Tsong-tai, my Guide, the Lama Mingyar Dondup, and the 13th Dalai Lama, now in one day within the space of a few hours I had been told one after the other was dying. Two already were dead, and the third . . . how long before he too went? A few days. I must make haste, I thought, and I turned and made my way from the inner temple into the main body of the lamasery. I went along the stone corridors towards the cell of the Abbot. As I was almost at the turning for his room I heard a sudden commotion and a thud. I hastened my footsteps.

Another lama, Jersi, also from Tibet, not from Lhasa but from Chambo, had had a telepathic message, too, by a different lama. He, too, had been urged to leave Chungking and to return with me as my attendant. He was a man who had studied motor vehicles and similar forms of transit. He had been rather too quick; immediately his messenger had departed he had jumped to his feet and raced down the stone corridor towards the Abbot's cell. He had not negotiated the corner but had slipped upon some butter which had been spilled from a lamp by a careless monk. He had slipped and fallen heavily. He broke a leg and an arm, and as I turned the corner I saw him lying there, gasping, with a shaft of bone protruding.

The Abbot came out of his cell at the noise. Together we knelt beside our fallen brother. The Abbot held his shoulder while I pulled on his wrist to set the broken bone. Then I called for splints and bandages, and soon Jersi was splinted and bandaged—arm and a leg. The leg was rather a different matter because it was a compound fracture, and we had to take him to his cell and apply traction. Then I left him in the care of another.

The Abbot and I went to his cell where I told him of the message I had received. I described to him the vision, and he, too, had had a similar impression. So it was agreed that I should leave the lamasery then, at that instant. The Abbot quickly sent for a messenger who went out at a run to get a horse, and to gallop full speed into Chungking on a mission. I stopped only to take food and to have food packed for me. I took spare blankets, and spare robe, then I made my way on foot down the path, past the clearing where earlier that evening I had had such a memorable experience, where I had seen for the last time my Guide, the Lama Mingyar Dondup. I walked on, feeling a sharp pang of emotion, fighting to control my feelings, fighting to maintain the imperturbable mien of a lama. So I came to the end of the path where it joined the road. I stood and waited.

Behind me, I thought, in the temple the deep bronze gongs would be calling the monks to service. The tinkle of the silver bells will punctuate the responses and the flutes and the trumpets will be sounding. Soon upon the night air came the throb of a powerful motor, and over the distant hill came the bright silver beams of headlamps. A racing car tore toward me and stopped with a squeal of tyres on the road. A man jumped out. "Your car, Honorable Lobsang Rampa. Shall I turn it first?" "No," I replied. "Go down the hill toward the left." I jumped in beside the driver. The monk who had been summoned by the Abbot had rushed off to Chungking to obtain a driver and powerful car. This was indeed a powerful vehicle, an immense black American monster. I sat beside the driver and we sped through the night on the road to Chengtu, two hundred miles from Chungking. Ahead of us great pools of light raced from the headlamps, showing up the unevenness of the road, illuminating the trees by the side, and making grotesque shadows as if daring us to catch them, as if urging us on faster and faster. The driver, Ejen, was a good driver, well trained, capable and safe. Faster and faster we went with the road a mere blur. I sat back, and thought and thought.

I had in my mind the thought of my beloved Guide, the Lama Mingyar Dondup, and the way he had trained me, all that he had done for me. He had been more to me than my own parents. I had in my mind also the thought of my beloved ruler, the 13th Dalai Lama, the last of His line, for the old prophecy said that the 13th Dalai Lama would pass, and with His passing would come a new order to Tibet. In 1950 the Chinese Communists began their invasion of Tibet, but before this the Communist Third Column had been in Lhasa. I thought of all this which I knew was going to happen, I knew this in 1933, I knew it before 1933 because it all followed exactly according to the prophecy.

So we raced on through the night two hundred miles to Chengtu. At Chengtu we got more petrol, we stretched our legs for ten minutes, and had food. Then on we went again, the wild drive through the night, through the darkness from Chengtu to Ya-an, a hundred miles further on, and there, as dawn was breaking, as the first streaks of light were shining in the sky, the road ended, the car could go no further. I went to a lamasery where by telepathy, the message had been received that I was on my way. A horse was ready, a high-spirited horse, one that kicked and reared, but in this emergency I had no time to pander to a horse. I got on, and stayed on, and the horse did my bidding as if it knew of the urgency of our mission. The groom released the bridle and off we shot, up the road, onwards, on the way to Tibet. The car would return to Chungking, the driver having the pleasure of a soft, speedy ride, while I had to sit in the high wooden saddle and ride on and on, changing horses after the end of a good run, changing always to high-spirited animals which had plenty of power because I was in a hurry.

There is no need to tell of the trials of that journey, the

bitter hardships of one solitary horseman. No need to tell of the crossing of the Yangtse river, and on to the Upper Salween. I raced on and on. It was gruelling work riding like this, but I made it in time. I turned through a pass in the mountains, and once again gazed upon the golden roofs of the Potala. I gazed upon the domes which hid the earthly remains of other bodies of the Dalai Lama, and I thought how soon would there be another dome concealing another body.

I rode on, and crossed again the Happy River. It was not happy for me this time. I crossed it and went along and I was in time. The hard, rushed journey had not been in vain. I was there for all the ceremonials and I took a very active part in them. There was, for me, a further unpleasant incident. A foreigner was there who wanted all consideration for himself. He thought that we were just natives, and that he was lord of all he surveyed. He wanted to be in the front of everything, noticed by all, and because I would not further his selfish aim—he tried to bribe a friend and me with wrist watches!—he has regarded me as an enemy ever since, and has indeed gone out of his way—has gone to extreme lengths—to injure me and mine. However, that has nothing to do with it, except that it shows how right were my Tutors when they warned me of jealousy.

They were very sad days indeed for us, and I do not propose to write about the ceremonial nor about the disposal of the Dalai Lama. It will suffice to say that his body was preserved according to our ancient method, and placed in a sitting position, facing the South as demanded by tradition. Time after time the head would turn toward the East. Many consider this to be a pointer from beyond death, saying that we must look toward the East. Well, the Chinese invaders came from the East to disrupt Tibet. That turning to the East was indeed a sign, a warning. If only we could have heeded it!

I went again to the home of my parents. Old Tzu had

107

died. Many of the people that I had known were changed. All was strange there. It was not a home to me. I was just a caller, a stranger, a high lama, a high dignitary of the temple who had returned temporarily from China. I was kept waiting to see my parents. At last I was conducted to them. Talk was forced, the atmosphere was strained. I was no longer a son of the house, but a stranger. But not quite a stranger in the sense that is usually meant, for my father conducted me to his private room, and there he took from its safe stronghold our Record, and carefully unwrapped it from its golden covering. Without a word I signed my name, the last entry. I signed my name, my rank, and my new qualifications as a qualified doctor and surgeon. Then the Book was solemnly re-wrapped and replaced in its hiding place beneath the floor. Together we returned to the room in which my mother and my sister sat. I made my farewells, and turned away. In the courtyard the grooms were holding my horse. I mounted and passed through the great gates for the last time. It was with a heavy heart that I turned into the Lingkhor Road and made my way to Menzekang, which is the main Tibetan hospital. I had worked here, and now I was paying a courtesy call to the huge old monk who was in charge, Chinrobnobo, I knew him well, a nice old man. He had taught me a lot after I had left Iron Hill Medical School. He took me into his room and asked me about Chinese medicine. I said, "They claim in China that they were the first to use acupuncture and moxibustion, but I know better. I have seen in the old records how these two remedies were brought from Tibet to be used in China years and years ago." He was most interested when I told him that the Chinese, and Western powers too, were investigating why these two remedies worked, because work they assuredly did. Acupuncture is a special method of inserting extremely fine needles into various parts of the body. They are so fine that no pain is felt. These needles are inserted, and they stimulate various healing reactions. They use

108

radium needles, and claim wonderful cures for it, but we of the East have used acupuncture for centuries with equal success. We have also used moxibustion. This is a method of preparing various herbs in a tube and igniting one end so that it glows red. This glowing end is brought near to a diseased skin and tissue, and in heating that area the virtue of the herbs passes direct to the tissues with curative effect. These two methods have been proved again and again, but how precisely they work has not been determined.

I looked again into the great storehouse in which were kept the many, many herbs, more than six thousand different types. Most of them unknown to China, unknown to the rest of the world. Tatura, for instance, which is the root of a tree, was a most powerful anaesthetic, and it could keep a person completely anaesthetised for twelve hours at a stretch, and, in the hands of a good practitioner, there would be no undesirable after effects whatever. I looked around, and I could find nothing with which to find fault in spite of all the modern advances of China and America. The old Tibetan cures still were satisfactory.

That night I slept in my old place, and as in the days when I was a pupil I attended the services. It all carried me back. What memories there were in every one of those stones! In the morning when it was light I climbed to the highest part of Iron Mountain, and gazed out over the Potala, over the Serpent Park, over Lhasa, and into the snow-clad mountains surrounding. I gazed long and then I went back into the Medical School and said my farewells and took my bag of tsampa. Then with my blanket rolled and my spare robe in front of me I remounted my horse and made my way down the hill.

The sun hid behind a black cloud as I reached the bottom of the path and passed by the village of Shë. Pilgrims were everywhere, pilgrims from all parts of Tibet, and from beyond, come to pay their respects at the Potala. Horoscope vendors were there crying their wares, and those who had magic potions and charms were doing a brisk trade. The recent ceremonials had brought merchants, traders, hawkers and beggars of all description to the Sacred Road. Nearby a yak train was coming in through the Western Gate, laden with goods for the markets of Lhasa. I stopped to watch, thinking that I might never again see this so familiar sight, and feeling sick at heart at the thought of leaving. There was a rustle behind me. "Your blessing, Honourable Medical Lama," said a voice, and I turned to see one of the Body Breakers, one of the men who had done so much to help me when, by order of the 13th Dalai Lama, he whose body I had just seen, I had studied with. When I had been able to get past the age-old tradition that bodies might not be dissected, I, because of my special task, had been given every facility to dissect bodies, and here was one of those men who had done so much to help me. I gave him my blessing, glad indeed that someone from the past recognised me. "Your teaching was wonderful," I said. "You taught me more than the Medical School of Chungking." He looked pleased, and put out his tongue to me in the manner of the serf. He backed away from me in the traditional manner, and mingled with the throng at the Gate.

For a few moments more I stood beside my horse, looking at the Potala, at the Iron Mountain, and then I went on my way, crossing the Kyi River, and passing many pleasant parks. The ground here was flat and green with the green of well-watered grass, a paradise twelve thousand eight hundred feet above sea level, ringed by mountains rising yet another six thousand feet, liberally speckled with lamaseries both large and small, and with isolated hermitages perched precariously on inaccessible rock spurs. Gradually the slope of the road increased, climbing to meet the mountain passes. My horse was fresh, well cared for and well fed. He wanted to hurry, I wanted to linger. Monks and merchants rode by, some of them looking at me curiously because I had departed from tradition and I was riding alone for greater speed. My father would never have ridden without an immense retinue as befitted his station, but I was of the modern age. So strangers looked at me curiously, but others whom I had known called a friendly greeting. At last my horse and I breasted the rise, and we came level with the great chorten of stones which was the last place from which Lhasa could be seen. I dismounted and tethered my horse, then sat on a convenient rock as I looked long into the valley.

The sky was a deep blue, the deep blue that is only seen at such altitudes. Snow-white clouds drifted lazily overhead. A raven flopped down beside me and pecked inquiringly at my robe. As an afterthought I added a stone as custom demanded to the huge pile beside me, the pile which had been built up by the work of centuries of pilgrims, for this was the spot from whence pilgrims obtained their first and last view of the Holy City.

Before me was the Potala, with its walls sloping inwards from the base. The windows, too, sloped from the bottom to the top, adding to the effect. It looked like a building carved by Gods from the living rock. My Chakpori stood even higher than the Potala, without dominating it. Further in I saw the golden roofs of the Jo Kang, the thirteen-hundred-year-old temple, surrounded by the administrative buildings. I saw the main road straight through, the willow grove, the swamps, the Snake Temple, and the beautiful patch which was the Norbu Linga, and the Lama's Gardens along by the Kyi Chu. But the golden roofs of the Potala were ablaze with light, catching the brilliant sunlight, and throwing it back with gold red rays, with every colour of the spectrum. Here, beneath these cupolas rested the remains of the Bodies of the Dalai Lama. The monument containing the remains of the 13th was the highest of the lot, some seventy feet—three stories high—and covered with a ton of purest gold. And inside that shrine were precious ornaments,

111

jewels, gold and silver, a fortune rested there beside the empty shell of its previous owner. And now Tibet was without a Dalai Lama, the last one had left, and the one yet to come, according to prophecy, would be one who would serve alien masters, one who would be in thrall of the Communists.

To the sides of the valley clung the immense lamaseries of Drepung, Sera, and Ganden. Half hidden in a clump of trees gleamed the white and gold of Nechung, the Oracle of Lhasa, the Oracle of Tibet. Drepung indeed looked like a rice heap, a white pile sprawled down the mountain side. Sera, known as the Wild Rose Fence, and Ganden the Joyous; I looked upon them and thought of the times I had spent within their walls, within their walled townships. I looked, too, at the vast number of smaller lamaseries, perched everywhere, up the mountain sides, in groves of trees; and I looked too at the hermitages dotted in places most difficult of access, and my thoughts went out to the men within, immured, perhaps, for life in darkness with no light at all, with food but once a day, in darkness, never to come out again in the physical, but by their special training able to move in the astral, able to see the sights of the world as a disembodied spirit. My gaze wandered; the Happy River meandered along through cuts and marshlands, hiding behind the skirts of trees, and reappearing in the open stretches. I looked and I saw the house of my parents, that large estate which had never been home to me. I saw pilgrims thronging the roads, making their circuits. Then from some distant lamasery I heard on the mild breeze the sound of the temple gongs, and the scream of the trumpets, and I felt a lump rising in my throat and a stinging sensation in the bridge of my nose. It was too much for me. I turned, and remounted my horse, and rode on, into the unknown.

I went on with the country becoming wilder, and wilder. I passed from pleasant parklands and sandy soil, and small homesteads, to rocky eminences, and wild gorges through which water rushed continuously filling the air with sound, drenching me to the skin with the spray. I rode on, staying the nights as before at lamaseries. This time I was a doubly welcome guest for I was able to give first hand information about the recent sad ceremonials at Lhasa, for I was one of the men there, one of the officials. We all agreed that it was the end of an era, a sad time would come upon our land. I was provided with ample food and fresh horses, and after days of travel I again arrived at Ya-an, where, to my joy, the big car was waiting with Jersi, the driver. Reports had filtered through that I was on my way, and the old Abbot at Chungking had thoughtfully sent it for me. I was glad indeed because I was saddlesore, and travel-stained, and weary. It was a pleasure indeed to see that gleaming great vehicle, the product of another science, a product which would bear me along swiftly, doing in hours what I would normally take days to accomplish. So I got in the car, thankful that the Abbot of the lamasery in Chungking was my friend and had so much thought for my comfort and my pleasure after the long arduous journey from my home in Lhasa. Soon we were speeding along the road to Changtu. There we stayed the night. There was no point in hurrying and getting back to Chungking in the small hours, so we stayed the night, and in the morning we looked around the place and did some local shopping. Then off we went again along the road to Chungking.

The red-faced boy was still at his plough, clad only in blue shorts. The plough drawn by the ungainly water buffalo. They wallowed through the mud trying to turn it over so that rice could be planted. We sped on faster, the birds overhead calling to one another, and making sudden swoops and darts as if for the sheer joy of living. Soon we were approaching the outskirts of Chungking. We were approaching along the road lined with the silver eucalyptus trees, with the limes, and the green pine trees. Soon we came to a little road at which I alighted and made my way on foot up the path to the lamasery. As I once again passed that clearing with the fallen tree and the trees lying at crazy angles I thought how memorable the events since I sat upon the bole and talked with my Guide, the Lama Mingyar Dondup. I stopped awhile in meditation, then I picked up my parcels once again and made my way on into the lamasery.

In the morning I went to Chungking and the heat was like a living thing, sweltering, stifling. Even the ricksha-pullers and the passengers who rode with them were looking wilted and jaded, in the intolerable heat. I, from the fresh air in Tibet, felt more than half dead, but I as a lama had to keep erect as an example to others. In the Street of the Seven Stars I came across friend Huang busy shopping, and I greeted him as the friend he was. "Huang," I said, "what are all these people doing here?" "Why, Lobsang," he answered, "people are coming from Shanghai. The trouble there with the Japanese is causing traders to shut up their shops and to come here to Chungking. I understand that some of the Universities are seriously thinking of it as well, and by the way," he went on, "I have a message for you. General (now Marshal) Feng Yu-hsiang wants to see you. He asked me to give you the message. Go and see him as soon as you return." "All right," I said, "how about you coming up with me?" He said that he would. We did our leisurely shopping, it was far too hot to hurry, and then we went back to the lamasery. An hour or two later we made our way up to the temple near where the General had his home, and there I saw him. He told me much about the Japanese, and the trouble they were making in Shanghai. He told me how the International Settlement there had recruited a police force of thugs and crooks who were not really trying to restore order. He said, "War is coming, Rampa, war is coming. We need all the doctors we can, and doctors who are also pilots. We must have them." He offered me a commission in the Chinese army, and gave me to understand that I could fly as much as I should like.

The General was an immense man, well over six feet tall, with broad shoulders and a huge head. He had been in many campaigns, and now he had thought, until the Japanese difficulty, that his days as a soldier were over. He was a poet, too, and he lived near the Temple for Viewing the 'Moon. I liked him, he was a man with whom I could get on, a clever man. Apparently, so he told me, one incident in particular had been sponsored by the Japanese to give them a pretext for invading China. Some Japanese monk had been killed by accident, and the Japanese authorities demanded that the mayor of Shanghai should prohibit the boycott of Japanese goods, disband the Association for National Deliverance, arrest the leaders of the boycott, and guarantee compensation for the killing of that monk. The Mayor, to preserve the peace and thinking of the overwhelming force of the Japanese, accepted the ultimatum on the 28th January, 1932. But at 10.30 that night, after the Mayor had actually accepted the ultimatum, the Japanese marines began occupying a number of streets in the International Settlement, and so paving the way for the next world war. This was all news to me. I knew nothing at all about it because I had been travelling elsewhere.

As we were talking a monk came, dressed in a grey-black gown, to tell us that the Supreme Abbot T'ai Shu was here, and we had to see him as well. I had to tell him about events in Tibet, about the last ceremonies of my beloved 13th Dalai Lama. He in turn told me of the grave fears which he and others had for the safety of China. "Not that we fear the final outcome," he said, "but the destruction, the death, and the suffering which will come first."

So they pressed me again to accept a commission in the Chinese forces, to place my training at their disposal. And then came the blow. "You must go to Shanghai," said the General. "Your services are very much needed there, and I suggest that your friend, Po Ku, goes with you. I have made preparations already, it is but for you, and he, to accept." "Shanghai?" I said. "That's a terrible place to be in. I really do not think much of it. However, I know that I must go, and so I will accept."

We talked on and on, and the evening shadows gradually crept in upon us, and the day turned to dusk, so that eventually we had to part. I rose to my feet, and made my way out into the courtyard, where the solitary palm was looking faded, and wilted in the heat, with its leaves hanging down, and turning brown. Huang was sitting patiently waiting for me, sitting immobile, wondering why the interview was so long. He, too, rose to his feet. Silently we made our way down the path, past the rushing gorge, and over the little stone bridge, down toward our own lamasery.

There was a large rock before the entrance to our path and we climbed upon it, where we could look out over the rivers. There was much activity nowadays. Little steamers were chugging along. Flames of smoke rising from their funnels being caught by the wind, were being blown out into a black banner. Yes, there were more steamers now than ever before I left for Tibet. Refugees were coming in, more every day, more traffic, people who could see into the future, and see what the invasion of China would really mean. There was more congestion in a city already congested.

As we looked up into the night sky we could see the great storm clouds piling up, and we knew that later in the night there would be a thunder-storm rolling down from the mountains, swamping the place with torrential rain, and deafening us with the echo and rumbles. Was this, we thought, a symbol of the troubles to come upon China? It certainly seemed so, the air was tense, electric. I think we both sighed in unison to think of the future of this land of which we were both so fond. But the night was upon us. The first heavy drops of the rainstorm were coming down and wetting us. We turned together, and made our way into the temple to where the Abbot was waiting for us, agog to be told all that had happened. I was glad indeed to see him, and to discuss matters, and to receive his praise for the course which I had agreed to undertake.

Far into the night we talked, and talked, deafened at times by the roaring thunder, and by the rushing of the rain upon the temple roof. Eventually we made our way to our beds upon the floor, and went to sleep. With the coming of the morning, after the first service, we made our preparations to set off again on the start of yet another phase of life, an even more unpleasant stage.

CHAPTER SIX

Clairvoyance

SHANGHAI! I had no illusions. I knew that Shanghai was going to be a very difficult spot indeed in which to live. But fate had decreed that I should go there, and so we made our preparations, Po Ku and I, and later in the morning we walked together down the street of steps, down to the docks, and went aboard a ship which would take us far down the river to Shanghai.

In our cabin—we shared a cabin—I lay upon my bunk, and thought of the past. I thought of the first time that I had known anything about Shanghai. It was when my Guide, the Lama Mingyar Dondup, was teaching me the finer points of clairvoyance, and as this particular knowledge may be of interest and help to many I will give the actual experience here.

It was a few years previously, when I was a student in one of the great lamaseries of Lhasa. I and others of my class were sitting in the schoolroom longing to be out. The class was worse than usual for the teacher was a great bore, one of our worst. The whole class was finding it difficult to follow his words and remain alert. It was one of those

117

days when the sun was shining warmly, when light fleecy clouds raced high overhead. Everything called us to go outside into the warmth and sunshine, away from musty classrooms and the droning voice of an uninteresting teacher. Suddenly there was commotion. Someone had come into the room. We, with our backs to the teacher, could not see who it was, and we dared not turn and look in case HE was looking at US! The rustle of paper, "Hmm, ruining my class." A sharp "crack" as the teacher brought his cane down on his desk, making all of us jump high with fright. "Lobsang Rampa, come here." Filled with foreboding I rose to my feet, turned and made my three bows. What had I done now? Had the Abbot seen me dropping pebbles on those visiting lamas? Had I been observed "sampling" those pickled walnuts? Had I—but the voice of the teacher soon put my mind at rest: "Lobsang Rampa, the Honourable Senior Lama, your Guide, Mingyar Dondup, requires you at once. Go, and pay more attention to him than you have to me!" I went, in a hurry.

Along the corridors, up the stairs, round to the right, and into the precincts of the lamas. "Tread softly here," I thought, "some crusty old dodderers along here. Seventh door left, that is it." Just as I raised my hand to knock, a voice said "Come in," and in I went. "Your clairvoyance never fails when there is food about. I have tea and pickled walnuts. You are just in time." The Lama Mingyar Dondup had not expected me so early, but now he certainly made me welcome. As we ate he talked. "I want you to study crystal gazing, using the various types of appliances. You must be familiar with them all."

After our tea he led me down to the storeroom. Here were kept the appliances of all kinds, planchettes, tarot cards, black mirrors, and a perfectly amazing range of devices. We wandered around, he pointing out various objects and explaining their use. Then, turning to me, he said, "Pick a crystal which you feel will be harmonious to you. Look at them all, and make your choice." I had had my eyes on a very beautiful sphere, genuine rock crystal without a flaw and of such a size that it needed two hands to hold it. I picked it up and said, "This is the one I want." My Guide laughed. "You have chosen the oldest and most valuable. If you can use it you can have it." This particular crystal, which I still have, had been found in one of the tunnels far below the Potala. In those unenlightened days it had been called "The Magic Ball" and given to the Medical Lamas of the Iron Mountain as it was considered to be connected with medicine.

A little later in this chapter I will deal with glass spheres, black mirrors, and water globes, but now it may be of interest to describe how we prepared to use the crystal, how we trained ourselves to become as one with it.

It is obvious that if one is healthy, physically and mentally fit, the sight is at its best. So it is with the Third Eye sight. One must be fit, and to that end we prepared before trying to use any of these devices. I had picked up my crystal, and now I looked at it. Held between my two hands it appeared to be a heavy globe which reflected upside-down a picture of the window, with a bird perched on the ledge outside. Looking more closely I could dimly see the reflection of the Lama Mingyar Dondup, and—yes—my own reflection as well. "You are looking at it, Lobsang, and that is not the way in which it is used. Cover it up and wait until you are shown."

The next morning I had to take herbs with my first meal, herbs to purify the blood and clear the head, herbs to tone up the constitution generally. Morning and night these had to be taken, for two weeks. Each afternoon I had to rest for an hour and a half with my eyes and the upper part of my head covered with a thick black cloth. During this time I had to practise special breathing to a particular rhythm pattern. I had to pay scrupulous attention to personal cleanliness during this time.

119

With the two weeks completed I went again to the Lama Mingyar Dondup. "Let us go to that quiet little room on the roof," he said. "Until you are more familiar with it you will need absolute quietness." We climbed the stairs, and emerged on the flat roof. To one side was a little house where the Dalai Lama had his audiences when he came to Chakpori for the Annual Blessing of the Monks. Now we were going to use it. *I* was going to, and that was indeed an honour, for no other than the Abbot and the Lama Mingyar Dondup could use it. Inside we sat on our cushion-seats on the floor. Behind us was a window through which one could see the distant mountains standing as the Guardians of our pleasant valley. The Potala too could be seen from here, but that was too familiar to bother about. I wanted to see what there was in the crystal. "Move around this way, Lobsang. Look at the crystal and tell me when all the reflections disappear. We must exclude all odd points of light. THEY are not what we want to see." That is one of the main points to remember. Exclude all light which causes reflections. Reflections merely distract the attention. Our system was to sit with the back to a north window, and draw a reasonably thick curtain across the window so as to provide a twilight. Now, with the curtains drawn, the crystal ball in my hands appeared dead, inert. No reflections at all marred its surface.

My Guide sat beside me. "Wipe the crystal with this damp cloth, dry it, then pick it up with this black cloth. Do not touch it with your hands yet." I did as instructed, carefully wiped the sphere, dried it, and picked it up with the black cloth which was folded into a square. My two hands I crossed, palms up, under the crystal which was thus supported in the palm of the left hand. "Now, look IN the sphere. Not AT it, but IN. Look at the very centre and then let your vision become blank. Do not try to see anything, just let your mind go blank." The latter was not difficult for me. Some of my teachers thought that my mind was blank all the time.

I looked at the crystal. My thoughts wandered. Suddenly the sphere in my hands seemed to grow, and I felt as if I was about to fall inside it. It made me jump, and the impression faded. Once more I held just a ball of crystal in my hands. "Lobsang! WHY did you forget all I told you? You were on the verge of seeing and your start of surprise broke the thread. You will see nothing today."

One has to look in the crystal and just hold one's mental focus on some inner part of it. Then there comes a peculiar sensation as if one is about to step inside another world. Any start or fright or surprise at this stage will spoil everything. The only thing to do then, while learning, of course, is to put aside the crystal and not attempt to "see" until one has had a night's sleep.

The next day we tried again. I sat, as before, with my back to the window, and saw to it that all disturbing facets of light were excluded. Normally I should have sat in the lotus attitude of meditation, but because of a leg injury this would not be the most comfortable for me. Comfort is essential. One must sit quite at ease. It is better to sit in an unorthodox manner and SEE, than to sit in one of the formal attitudes and see nothing. Our rule was, sit any way you like so long as it is comfortable, as discomfort will distract the attention.

Into the crystal I gazed. By my side the Lama Mingyar Dondup sat motionless, erect, as if carved from stone. What would I see? That was my thought. Would it be the same as when I first saw an aura? The crystal looked dull, inert. "I'll never see in this thing," I thought. It was evening so that there would be no strong play of sunlight to cause shifting shadows, so that the clouds would not temporarily obscure the light, and then permit it to shine brightly. No shadows, no points of light. It was twilight in the room and with the black cloth between my hands and the sphere

121

I could see no reflections at all on its surface. But I was supposed to be looking inside.

Suddenly the crystal seemed to come alive. Inside a fleck of white appeared at the centre and spread like white swirling smoke. It was as if a tornado raged inside, a silent tornado. The smoke thickened and thinned, thickened and thinned, and then spread in an even film over the globe. It was like a curtain designed to prevent me from seeing. I probed mentally, trying to force my mind past the barrier. The globe seemed to swell, and I had a horrid impression of falling head first into a bottomless void. Just then a trumpet blared and the white curtain shivered into a snowstorm which melted as if in the heat of the noonday sun.

"You were near it then, Lobsang, very near." "Yes, I would have seen something if that trumpet had not been sounded. It put me off." "Trumpet? Oh, you were as far as that, eh? That was your subconscious trying to warn you that clairvoyance and crystal gazing are for the very few. Tomorrow we will go further."

On the third evening my Guide and I sat together as before. Once again he reminded me of the rules. This third evening was more successful. I sat with the sphere lightly held and concentrated on some invisible point in its dim interior. The swirling smoke appeared almost at once and soon provided a curtain. I probed with my mind, thinking, "I am going through, I am going through NOW!" Again came the horrid impression of falling. This time I was prepared. Down from some immense height I plummeted, falling straight towards the smoke-covered world which was growing with amazing rapidity. Only strict training prevented me from screaming as I approached the white surface at tremendous speed—and passed through, unharmed.

Inside the sun was shining. I looked about me in very real astonishment. I had died surely for this was nowhere that I knew. What a strange place! Water, dark water, stretched before me as far as I could see. More water than

I had ever imagined existed. Some distance away a huge monster like a fearsome fish forced its way across the surface of the water. In the middle a black pipe sent what looked like smoke upwards, to be blown back by the wind. To my amazement I saw what appeared to be little people walking about on the "fish's back!" This was too much for me. I turned to flee—and stopped in my tracks petrified. This was too much. Great stone houses many stories high were before me. Just in front of me a Chinaman dashed pulling a device on two wheels. Apparently he was a carrier of some sort, because on the wheeled thing a woman was perched. "She must be a cripple," I thought, "and has to be carried about on wheels." Towards me a man was walking, a Tibetan lama. I held my breath, it was exactly like the Lama Mingyar Dondup when he was many years younger. He walked straight up to me, through me, and I jumped with fright. "Oh!" I wailed, "I'm blind." It was dark, I could not see. "It is all right, Lobsang, you are doing well. Let me draw back the curtains." My Guide did so, and into the room flooded the pale light of evening.

"You certainly have very great clairvoyance powers, Lobsang; they merely need directing. Quite inadvertently I touched the crystal and from your remarks I gather that you have seen the impression of when I went to Shanghai many years ago, and nearly collapsed at my first sight of steamer and ricksha. You are doing well."

I was still in a daze, still living in the past. What strange and terrible things there were outside of Tibet. Tame fishes which belched smoke and upon which one rode, men who carried wheeled women, I was afraid to think of it, afraid to dwell on the fact that I too would have to go to that strange world later.

"Now you must immerse the crystal in water to erase the impression you have just seen. Dip it right in, allow it to rest on a cloth on the bottom of the bowl, and then lift it out with another cloth. Do not let your hands touch it yet."

That is an important point to remember when using a crystal. One should always demagnetise it after each reading. The crystal becomes magnetised by the person holding it in much the same way as a piece of iron will become magnetised if brought into contact with a magnet. With the iron it is usually sufficient to knock it to cause it to lose its magnetism, but a crystal should be immersed in water. Unless one does demagnetise after each reading the results become more and more confusing. The "auric emanations" of succeeding people begin to build up and one gives a completely inaccurate reading.

No crystal should ever be handled by anyone except the owner, other than for the purpose of "magnetising" for a reading. The more the sphere is handled by other people, the less responsive it becomes. We were taught that when we had given a number of readings in a day we should take the crystal to bed with us so that we should personally magnetise it by its being close to us. The same result would be attained by carrying the crystal around with us, but we would look rather foolish ambling around twiddling the crystal ball!

When not in use, the crystal should be covered by a black cloth. One should NEVER allow strong sunlight to fall on it, as that impairs its use for esoteric purposes. Nor should one ever allow a crystal to be handled by a mere thrill-seeker. There is a purpose behind this. A thrill-seeker not being genuinely interested but wanting cheap entertainment, harms the aura of the crystal. It is much the same as handing an expensive camera or watch to a child so that its idle curiosity may be appeased.

Most people could use a crystal if they would take the trouble to find what type suited them. We make sure that our spectacles suit us. Crystals are equally important. Some persons can see better with a rock crystal, and some with glass. Rock crystal is the most powerful type. Here is a brief history of mine as recorded at Chakpori.

Millions of years ago volcanoes belched out flame and lava. Deep in the earth various types of sand were churned together by earthquakes, and fused into a kind of glass by the volcanic heat. The glass was broken into pieces by the earthquakes and spewed out over the mountain-sides. Lava, solidified, covered much of it.

In the course of time rock falls exposed some of this natural glass, or "rock crystal." One piece was seen by tribal priests in the dawn of human life. In those far off days the priests were men who had occult power, who could predict, and tell the history of an object by psychometry. Such a one must have touched one particular fragment of crystal and been impressed enough to take it home. There must have been a clear spot from which he gained clairvoyant impressions. Laboriously he and others chipped the fragment into a sphere, as that was the most convenient to hold. From generation to generation, for centuries, it was passed from priest to priest, each charged with the task of polishing the hard material. Slowly the sphere became rounder and clearer. For an age it was worshipped as the Eye of a God. In the Age of Enlightenment it came into its own as an instrument whereby the Cosmic Consciousness could be tapped. Now, almost four inches across and as clear as water, it was carefully packed and hidden in a stone casket in a tunnel far beneath the Potala.

Centuries later it was discovered by monk explorers and the inscription on the casket was deciphered. "This is the Window of the Future," it read, "the crystal in which those who are fitted can see the past and know the future. It was in the custody of the High Priest of the Temple of Medicine." As such, the crystal was taken to Chakpori, the present Temple of Medicine, and kept for a person who could use it. I was that person, for me it lives.

Rock crystal of such size is rare, doubly rare when it is without flaw. Not everyone can use such a crystal. It may be too strong and tend to dominate one. Glass spheres can be

125

obtained, and those are useful for gaining the necessary preliminary experience. A good size is from three to four inches; size is NOT important at all. Some monks have a tiny sliver of crystal set in a large finger-ring. The important point is to be sure that there are no flaws, or that there is only a slight defect that is not at all visible in subdued lighting. Small crystals, of "rock" or glass have the advantage of light weight, and that is considerable when one tends to hold the sphere.

A person who desires to purchase a crystal of any type should advertise in one of the "psychic" papers. The things offered for sale at certain shops are more suitable for conjurors or stage turns. Usually there are blemishes which do not show until one has bought the thing and taken it home! Have any crystal sent on approval, and as soon as you unpack it wash it in running water. Carefully dry it, and then examine it, holding it with a dark cloth. The reason? Wash it to remove any fingermarks which may appear to be faults, and hold it so that YOUR fingerprints do not mislead you.

You cannot expect to sit down, look in the crystal, and "see pictures." Nor is it fair to blame the crystal for your failure. It is merely an instrument, and you would not blame a telescope if you looked through the wrong end and saw only a small picture.

Some people cannot use a crystal. Before giving up they should try a "black mirror." This can be made very cheaply indeed by procuring a large lamp glass from a motor accessory shop. The glass must be concave and quite smooth and plain. The ridged type of car headlamp glass is not suitable. With a suitable glass hold the outer curved surface over a candle flame. Move it about so that there is an even deposit of soot on the OUTER surface of the glass. This can be "fixed" with some cellulose lacquer such as is used to prevent brass from tarnishing.

With the black mirror ready, proceed as you would with

the round crystal. Suggestions applicable to any type of "crystal" are given later in this chapter. With the black mirror one looks at the INNER surface, being careful to exclude all random reflections.

Another type of black mirror is the one known to us as "null." It is the same as the former mirror, but the soot is on the INSIDE of the curve. A big disadvantage is that one cannot "fix" the soot, as to do so would be to provide a glossy surface. This mirror may be of more use to those who are distracted by reflections.

Some people use a bowl of water and gaze into it. The bowl must be clear, and entirely without pattern. Place a dark cloth under it, and it becomes in effect a glass crystal. In Tibet there is a lake so situated that one sees, yet almost doesn't see the water in it. It is a famous lake and is used by the State Oracles in some of their most important pre- dictions. This lake, we call it Chö-kor Gyal-ki Nam-tso (in English, The Heavenly Lake of the Victorious Wheel of Religion) is at a place called Tak-po, some hundred miles from Lhasa. The district around is mountainous and the lake is enclosed by high peaks. The water is normally very blue indeed, but at times as one looks from certain vantage points the blue changes to a swirling white, as if whitewash had been dropped in. The water swirls and foams, then suddenly a black hole appears in the middle of the lake, while above it dense white clouds form. In the space between the black hole and the white clouds a picture of the future events can be seen.

To this spot, at least once in his lifetime, comes the Dalai Lama. He stays at a nearby pavilion and looks at the lake. He sees events important to him and, not least im- portant, the date and manner of his passing from this life. Never has the lake been proved wrong!

We cannot all go to that lake, but most of us with a little patience and faith can use a crystal. For Western readers here is a suggested method. The word "crystal" will cover rock crystal, glass, black mirrors, and the water globe.

For a week pay particular attention to the health. For this week in particular avoid (as much as possible in this troubled world) worries and anger. Eat sparingly and take no sauces or fried foods. Handle the crystal as much as possible without making any attempt to "see." This will transfer some of your personal magnetism to it, and enable you to become quite familiar with the feel of it. Remember to cover the crystal at all times when you are not handling it. If you can, keep it in a box which can be locked. This will prevent other people from playing with it in your absence. Direct sunlight, as you know, should be avoided.

After the seven days take the crystal to a quiet room with a north light if possible. The evening is the best time, as then there is no direct sunlight to wax and wane with the passing of clouds.

Sit—in any attitude you find comfortable—with your back to the light. Take the crystal into your hands and note any reflections on its surface. These must be eliminated by drawing the curtains across the window, or by changing your position.

When you are satisfied hold the crystal in contact with the centre of your forehead for a few seconds, and then slowly withdraw it. Now hold it in your cupped hands, the back of which can rest on your lap. Gaze idly at the surface of the crystal, then move your vision inwards to the centre, to what you must imagine as a zone of nothingness. Just let your mind go blank. Avoid trying to see anything. Avoid any strong emotion.

Ten minutes is enough for the first night. Gradually increase the time, until at the end of the week you can do it for half an hour.

The next week let your mind go blank as soon as you can. Just gaze into nothingness inside the crystal. You should find that its outlines waver. It may appear that the whole sphere is growing, or you may feel that you are falling forward. That is how it should be. Do NOT start with astonishment, for if you do it will prevent you from "seeing" for the rest of the evening. The average person "seeing" for the first time jerks in much the same way as we sometimes jerk when we are falling off to sleep.

With a little more practice you will find that the crystal is apparently growing larger and larger. One evening you will find as you look in that it is luminous and filled with a white smoke. This will clear—provided you do not jerk —and you will have your first view of the (usually) past. It will be something connected with you, for only you have handled the sphere. Keep on at it, seeing just your own affairs. When you can "see" at will, direct it to show what you want to know. The best method is to say to yourself firmly, and out loud. "I am going to see so-and-so tonight." If you believe it, you WILL see what you desire. It is as simple as that.

To know the future you must marshal your facts. Gather all the data you have available, and say them to yourself. Then "ask" the crystal, and tell yourself that you are going to see what you want to know.

A warning here. One cannot use the crystal for personal gain, to forecast the result of races, nor to injure another person. There is a powerful occult law which will make it all recoil on your own head if you try to exploit the crystal. That law is as inexorable as time itself.

By now you should have been able to obtain much practice in your own affairs. Would you like to try on someone else? Dip the crystal in water and carefully dry it without touching the surface. Then hand it to the other person. Say, "Take it in your two hands and THINK what you want to know. Then pass it back to me." Naturally you will have warned your enquirer not to speak or disturb you. It is advisable to try with some well-known friend first as strangers often prove disconcerting when one is learning.

When your enquirer passes back the crystal you will take

it in your hands, either bare or covered in the black cloth, it does not matter which; you should have "personalised" the crystal by now. Settle yourself comfortably, raise the crystal to your forehead for a second, then let your hands rest on your lap, supporting the crystal in any way which causes no strain. Look INTO it and let your mind become blank, quite blank if you can, but this first attempt may be somewhat difficult if you are self-conscious.

As you compose yourself, if you have trained yourself as suggested, you will observe one of three things. They are true pictures, symbols, and impressions. True pictures should be your aim. Here the crystal clouds, and then the clouds disperse to show actual pictures, living pictures of what you want to know. There is no difficulty in interpreting in such a case.

Some people do not see true pictures; they see symbols. They may see, as an example, a row of X's, or a hand. It may be a windmill, or a dagger. Whatever it is you will soon learn to interpret them correctly.

The third thing is impressions. Here nothing is seen except swirling clouds and a little luminescence, but as the crystal is held, definite impressions are felt or heard. It is essential to avoid personal bias, essential not to over-rule the crystal by one's own personal feelings about a certain case.

The true Seer never tells a person of the date or even the probability of death. You will know, but you should NEVER tell. Nor will you warn a person of impending illness. Say instead: "It is advisable to take a little more care than usual on such-and-such a date)." And never tell a person: "Yes, your husband is out with a girl who —etc., etc." If you are using the crystal correctly you will KNOW that he IS out, but is he out on business? Is she a relation? Never, NEVER tell anything that would tend to break up a home or cause unhappiness. This is abuse of the crystal. Use it only for good, and in return good will come to you. If you see nothing, say so, and the enquirer will respect you. You can "invent" what you say you see, and perhaps you say something which the enquirer KNOWS to be incorrect. Then your prestige and reputation are gone, and you also bring a bad name to occult science.

Having given your reading to the enquirer carefully wrap up the crystal and set it down gently. When the enquirer has left you are advised to dip the crystal in water, wipe it dry, and then handle it to re-personalise it with your own magnetism. The more you handle the crystal the better it will be. Avoid scratching it, and when you have finished, put it away in the black cloth. If you can, put it in a box and lock it. Cats are great offenders, some of them will sit for a very long time "gazing." And when you use the crystal next time, you do not want to see the cat's life history and ambitions. It CAN be done. In Tibet in some of the "occult" lamasaries a cat is questioned by the crystal when it comes off duty after guarding gems. Then the monks know if there has been any attempt at stealing.

It is strongly advised that before embarking on any form of training in crystal gazing, you enquire most thoroughly into your secret motives. Occultism is a two-edged weapon, and those who "play" out of idle curiosity are sometimes punished by mental or nervous disorders. You can know through it the pleasure of helping others, but you can also know much that is horrible and unforgettable. It is safer just to read this chapter unless you are very, very sure of your motives.

Once having decided on the crystal do not change it. Make a definite habit to touch it every day, or every other day. The Saracens of old would never show a sword, even to a friend, unless to draw blood. If for some reason they HAD to show the weapon, then they pricked a finger to "draw blood." So with the crystal, if you show it at all to anyone, READ it even though it be only your own affair. Read it, although you need not tell anyone what you are

131

doing or what you see. This is not superstition, but a sure way of training yourself so that when the crystal is uncovered you "see" automatically, without preparation, without thinking about it.

CHAPTER SEVEN

Mercy Flight

GENTLY the boat slid to a halt in Soochow Creek. Chinese coolies swarmed aboard, yelling madly and gesticulating. Quickly our goods were removed, and we got in a ricksha and were conveyed swiftly along the Bund to the Chinese city to a temple at which I was to stay for the time being. Po Ku and I were silent in a world of babel. Shanghai was a very noisy place indeed, and a busy one too. Busier than normal because the Japanese were trying to make grounds for a fierce attack, and for some time past they had been searching foreign residents who wanted to cross the Marco Polo Bridge. They were causing extreme embarrassment by the thoroughness of their search. Western people could not understand that the Japanese, or the Chinese either, could see no shame in the human body, but only in people's thoughts about the human body, and when Westerners were being searched by the Japanese they thought it was meant as a deliberate insult, which it was not.

For a time I had a private practice in Shanghai, but to the Easterner "time" is of no account. We do not say such-and-such a year, for all times flow into one. I had a private practice, doing medical and psychological work. There were patients to see in my office, and in the hospitals. Of leisure there was none. Any time free from medical work was taken up by intensive studies of navigation, and the theory of flight. Long hours after nightfall I flew above the twinkling lights of the city, and out over the countryside with only the faintest glimmers from peasants' cottages to guide me.

The years rolled on unheeded, I was much too busy to bother about dates. The Shanghai Municipal Council knew me well and made full use of my professional services. I had a good friend in a White Russian. Bogomoloff was one who had escaped from Moscow during the revolution. He had lost all in that tragic time, and now he was employed by the Municipal Council. He was the first white man whom I had been able to know and I knew him thoroughly—a man indeed.

He could see quite clearly that Shanghai had no defences against aggression. Like us, he could foresee the horrors that were to come.

On the 7th July, 1937, there was an incident at the Marco Polo Bridge. The incident has been written about far too much, and I am not going to keep on repeating it. The incident was notable only for being the actual starting-point of war between China and Japan. Now things were on a war-time basis. Hard times were upon us. The Japanese were aggressive, truculent. Many of the foreign traders, and the Chinese in particular, had foreseen the coming trouble, and they had moved themselves and their families, and their goods to various parts of China, to the inland parts such as Chungking. But peasants in the outlying districts of Shanghai had come pouring into the city, thinking, for some reason, they would be safe, apparently believing in safety in numbers.

Through the streets of the city, by day and by night, poured lorries of the International Brigade, loaded with mercenaries of many different countries, charged with keeping peace in the city itself. All too often they were just plain murderers who had been recruited for their brutality. If there had been any incident at all which they did not like, they would come out in force, and without any warning, without any provocation or cause, they would loosen

133

off their machine guns, rifles, and their revolvers, killing harmless and innocent civilians, and more often than not doing nothing at all against guilty persons. We used to say in Shanghai that it was far better to deal with the Japanese than with the red-faced barbarians, as we called certain members of the International Police Force.

For some time I had been specialising with women, treating them as a physician and as a surgeon, and I had a very satisfactory practice indeed in Shanghai. The experience I gained in those pre-active war days was going to stand me in good stead later.

Incidents were becoming more and more frequent. Reports were coming in of the horrors of the Japanese invasion. Japanese troops and supplies were absolutely pouring into the country, into China. They were ill-treating the peasants, robbing, raping, as they always did. At the end of 1938 the enemy were on the outskirts of the city; the ill-armed Chinese forces fought truly valiantly. They fought to the death. Few indeed there were to be driven back by the Japanese hordes. The Chinese fought as only those who are defending their homeland could fight, but they were overwhelmed by sheer weight of numbers. Shanghai was declared an open city in the hope that the Japanese would respect the conventions and not bomb the historic place. The city was quite undefended, there were no guns, no weapons of any kind. The military forces were withdrawn. The city was crammed with refugees. The old population had mostly gone. The universities, centres of learning and culture, the big firms, the banks, and others, they had been moved to places like Chungking and to other remote districts. But in their place had come refugees, people of all nations and stations, fleeing from the Japanese, thinking that there was safety in numbers. Air raids were becoming more and more frequent, but people were becoming a little hardened to them, a little used to them. Then one night the Japanese really bombed the city. Every

134

plane they could get in the air took off, even fighter planes had bombs attached to them, and the pilots also had grenades in the cockpits to toss over the sides. The night sky became thick with planes, flying in formation across a defenceless city, flying like a swarm of locusts, and like a swarm of locusts they cleared everything in their path. Bombs were dropping everywhere, indiscriminately. The city was a sea of flames, and there was no defence; we had nothing with which to defend ourselves.

Around midnight I was walking down a road at the height of the uproar. I had been attending a case, a dying woman. Now metal was raining down, and I wondered where to shelter. Suddenly there was a faint whistle, growing to a whine, and then to the blood-curdling screech of a falling bomb. There was a sensation as if all sound, as if all life, had stopped. There was an impression of nothingness, of utter blank. I was picked up as if by a giant hand, twirled about in the air, tossed up in the air, and flung violently. For some minutes I lay half stunned, with hardly any breath in me, wondering if I were already dead and waiting to continue my journey to the other world. Shakily I picked myself up, and stared about me in absolute stupefaction. I had been walking down a road between two rows of tall houses; now I was standing on a desolate plain with no houses at all on on either side, just piles of shattered rubble, piles of thin dust bespattered by blood and parts of human bodies. The houses had been crowded, and the heavy bomb had dropped. It had been so close to me that I had been in the partial vacuum, and for some extraordinary reason I had heard no sound, and had come to no harm. The carnage was simply appalling. In the morning we piled the bodies house high and burned them, burned them to prevent the spread of plague, because under the hot sun the bodies were already decomposing, turning green and swelling. For days we dug beneath the rubble, trying to save any that might be alive, digging out those who were dead, and burning

135

them on the spot in an attempt to save the city from disease.

Late one afternoon I was in an old part of Shanghai. I had just crossed a slanting bridge astraddle a canal. To my right, under a street booth, were some Chinese astrologers and fortune-tellers, sitting at their counters, reading the future for avid customers who were anxious to know if they would survive the war, and if conditions would improve. I looked at them, mildly amused to think that they really believed what these moneymakers were telling them. The fortune-tellers were going by rote through the characters which surrounded the customer's name on a board, telling them of the outcome of the war, telling the women of the safety of their men. A little further on other astrologers— perhaps taking a rest from their professional duties!—were acting as public scribes; they were writing letters for people to send to other parts of China, giving the news, possibly, of family affairs. They made a precarious living writing for those who could not write, and they did it in the open; anyone who cared to stop could listen and know about the private business of the family. In China there is no privacy. The street scribe used to shout out in a very loud voice what he was writing, so that prospective customers should understand how beautifully he phrased his letters. I continued my walk to a hospital where I was going to do some operations. I went on past the booth of the sellers of incense, past the shops of the second-hand booksellers, who always seem to congregate on the waterside, and who, as in most cities, displayed their wares at the edge of a river. Further on were the vendors of incense and of temple objects, such as the statues of the Gods Ho Tai and of Kuan Yin, the first being the God of Good Living, and the second being the Goddess of Compassion. I went on to the hospital, and I did my allotted tasks. Later I returned by the same road. The Japanese had been over with their bombers; bombs had dropped. No longer were there booths or bookshops. No longer were there sellers of objects, or of incense, for

136

they and their goods had returned to dust. Fires were raging, buildings were crumbling, so again it was ashes to ashes and dust to dust.

But Po Ku and I had other things to do besides stay in Shanghai. We were going to investigate the possibility of starting an air ambulance service on the direct orders of General Chiang Kai-Shek. I well remember one in particular of these flights. The day was chilly, white fleecy clouds raced overhead. From somewhere over the skyline came the monotonous CRUMP-CRUMP-CRUMP of Japanese bombs. Occasionally there was the far-off drone of aero engines, like the sounds of bees on a hot summer's day. The rough rugged road beside which we sat had borne the weight of many feet that day, and for many days past. Peasants trudged by in an attempt to escape from the senseless cruelty of the power-mad Japanese. Old peasants almost at the end of their life-span, pushing along one-wheeled barrows with all their worldly possessions upon them. Peasants bowed down almost to the ground, carrying on their backs almost all they had. Ill-armed troops were going the other way, with scanty equipment loaded on to ox-carts. They were men going blindly to their death, trying to stop the ruthless advance, trying to protect their country, their homes. Going on blindly not knowing why they had to go on, not knowing what caused the war.

We crouched beneath the wing of an old tri-motored plane, an old plane that had already been worn out before it reached our eager and uncritical hands. Dope was peeling from the canvas-covered wings. The wide undercarriage had been repaired and strengthened with split bamboos, and the tail skid was re-shod with the broken end of a car spring. Old Abie, as we called her, had never failed us yet. Her engines sometimes stopped, it is true, but only one at a time. She was a high-winged monoplane of a rather famous American make. She had a wooden fabric-covered body, and streamlining was a term unknown when she was made.

137

The modest speed of 120 miles an hour felt at least twice as fast. Fabric drummed, spars creaked and protested, and the wide open exhaust added to the clamour.

A long time ago she had been doped white with huge red crosses on her side and wings. Now she was sadly streaked and marred. Oil from the engines had added a rich ivory-yellow patina making her look like an old Chinese carving. Petrol overflowing and blowing back contributed other hues, while the various patches added from time to time gave quite a bizarre appearance to the old plane.

Now the racket of crumps had died down. Another Japanese raid was over, and our work was just starting. Once again we checked our meagre equipment; saws, two, one large and one small and pointed; knives, assorted, four. One of them was an ex-butcher's carver, one was a photographic retouching knife. The other two were authentic scalpels.

Forceps, few in number. Two hypodermic syringes with woefully blunt needles. One aspirating syringe with rubber tubing, and medium trocher. Straps, yes, we must be very sure of them. With no anaesthetics we often had to strap our patients down.

It was Po Ku's turn turn to fly today, and mine to sit in the back and watch for Japanese fighters. Not for us the luxury of an intercom. We had a length of string, one end tied to the pilot, the other jerked by the observer in a crude code.

Warily I swung the propellers, for Abie had a strong backfire. One by one the engines coughed, spat a gout of oily black smoke, and awoke to strident life. Soon they warmed and settled down to a fairly rhythmic roar. I climbed aboard, and made my way to the stern where we had made an observation window in the fabric. Two yanks of the cord and Po Ku was informed that I was safe in position, squatting on the floor, forced in between the struts, crammed. The engine roar increased, and the whole plane

138

shuddered, and moved away down the field. There was a rumbling scrunch of the landing gear, and the creak of twisting woodwork. The tail bobbed, and dipped as we hit ridges. I was bounced from floor to roof. I settled myself even more tightly because I felt like a pea in a pod. With a final thud and clatter the old plane climbed into the air, and the noise became less as the engines were throttled back. A vicious yaw and dip as we hit raising air just clear of the trees, and my face was nearly forced through the observation window. Violent little jerks on the string from Po Ku meaning, "Well, we've made it once again. Are you still there?" My answering jerks as expressive as I could make them, indicating what I thought of his take-off.

Po Ku could see where we were going. I could see what we had just left. This time we were going to a village in the Wuhu district where there had been heavy raids, and many, many casualties, and no assistance on the spot. We always took turns flying the plane, and acting as observer. Abie had many blind spots, and the Japanese fighters were very fast. Often their speed saved us. We could slow down to a mere fifty when we were not heavily laden, and the average Japanese pilot had no skill at shooting. We used to say that we were safer right in front of them, because they always missed what was in front of their squat noses!

I kept a good lookout, on the alert for hated "blood-spots" which, aptly, were the Japanese planes. The Yellow River passed beneath our tail plane. The cord jerked three times. "We are landing," signalled Po Ku. Up went the tail, the roar of the engines died and was replaced by a pleasant "wick-wick, wick-wick" as the propellers idly turned over. We glided down with motors throttled well back. Creaks from the rudder as we turned slightly to correct our course. Flaps and tremors from the fabic covering as it vibrated in the wide breeze. A sudden short burst from the engines, and the jarring clatter and rumble as we touched down, and rumbled once again from ridge to ridge. Then the

139

moment most hated by the unfortunate observer cramped in the tail; the moment when the tail dropped and the metal shoe ploughed through the parched earth, raising clouds of choking dust, dust laden with particles of human excreta which the Chinese use to ferilize the fields.

I unfolded my bulky figure from the cramped space in the tail, and stood up with groans of pain as my circulation started to work again. I climbed up the sloping fuselage towards the door. Po Ku had already got it open, and we dropped to the ground. Running figures came racing up to us. "Come quickly, we have many casualties. General Tien had a metal bar blown through him, and it is sticking out back and front."

In the wretched hovel that was being used as an emergency hospital the General sat bolt upright, his normally yellow skin now a drab grey-green from pain and fatigue. From just above the left inguinal canal a bright steel bar protruded. It looked like the rod used to operate car jacks. Whatever it really was, it had been blown through his body by the blast of a near-miss bomb. Certainly I had to remove it with the least possible delay. The end emerging from the back, just above the left sacro-iliac crest, was smooth and blunt, and I considered that it had just missed or pushed aside, the descending colon.

After careful examination of the patient I took Po Ku outside, out of hearing of those within, and sent him to the plane on a somewhat unusual mission. While he was away I carefully cleansed the General's wounds, and the metal bar. He was small and old, but in fair physical condition. We had no anaesthetics, I told him, but I would be as gentle as possible. "I shall hurt you, no matter how careful I am," I said. "But I will do my best." He was not worried. "Go ahead," he said. "If nothing is done I shall die anyhow, so I have nothing to lose, but all to gain."

From the lid of a supply box I prised off a piece of wood, about eighteen inches square, and made a hole in the centre

140

so that it was a tight fit on the metal rod. By this time Po Ku had returned with the plane's tool kit, such as it was. We carefully threaded the board onto the bar, and Po Ku held it tightly against the patient's body. I gripped the bar with our large Stillson wrench, and pulled gently. Nothing happened, except that the unfortunate patient turned white.

"Well," I thought, "we can't leave the wretched thing as it is, so it is kill or cure." I braced my knee against Po Ku, who was holding the board in position, took a fresh grip of the bar, and pulled hard, rotating gently. With a horrid sucking sound the rod came free, and I, off my balance, fell on the back of my head. Quickly I picked myself up, and we hastened to the General and staunched the flow of blood. Peering into the wound with the aid of a flashlight I came to the conclusion that no great damage had been done, so we stitched and cleaned where we could reach. By now, after taking stimulants, the General was looking a much better colour and—as he said—feeling a lot happier. He was now able to lie on his side, whereas before he had had to sit bolt upright, bearing the weight of that heavy metal bar. I left Po Ku to finish the dressing, and went to the next case, a woman who had her right leg blown off just above the knee. A tournique had been applied too tightly and for too long. There was only one thing that could be done; we had to amputate the stump.

We had men tear down a door, and on it we strapped the woman. Quickly I cut around the flesh in a "vee," with the point toward the body. With a fine saw I reached in and severed the bone as high as possible. Then carefully folding the two flaps together I stitched them to form a cushion with the end of the bone. Just over half-an-hour it took, half-an-hour of sheer agony, and all the time the woman was quiet, she made no sound, not the slightest whimper, nor did she flinch. She knew that she was in the hands of friends. She knew that what we did, we did for her good.

141

There were other cases. Minor injuries, and major ones too, and by the time they had been dealt with it was getting dark. Today it had been Po Ku's turn to fly, to be pilot, but he was quite unable to see in the fading light, and so I had to take over.

We hurried back to the plane, packing away our equipment with loving care. Once again it had served us well. Then Po Ku swung the propellers and started the motors. Stabbing blue-red flames came from our open exhaust, and we must have looked like a fire-eating dragon to one who had never before seen a plane. I clambered aboard, and dropped into the pilot's seat, so tired that I could hardly keep my eyes open. Po Ku tottered in after me, shut the door, and fell asleep on the floor. I waved to the men outside to pull away the big stones chocking the wheels.

It was getting darker and the trees were very hard to see. I had memorised the lie of the land, and raced up the starboard engine to turn us round. There was no wind. Then facing what I hoped was the right direction I opened all three throttles as wide as they could be opened. The engines roared, and the plane trembled and clattered as we moved off, swaying with ever-increasing speed. The instruments were invisible. We had no lights, and I knew that the unseen end of the field was frighteningly close. I pulled back on the control column. The plane rose, faltered and dipped, and rose again. We were airborne. I banked and we turned in a lazy circle, climbing. Just below the cold, night clouds I levelled off, looking for our plain landmark, the Yellow River. There it was off to the left, showing a faint sheen against the darker earth. I watched, too, for any other aircraft in the sky, because I was defenceless. With Po Ku asleep on the floor behind me I had no one to keep a watch from the rear.

Settled on our course I leant back, thinking how astonishingly tiring these emergency trips could be, having to improvise, to make do, and patch up poor bleeding bodies with anything that came to hand. I thought of the fabulous tales I had heard of hospitals in England and America, and of the immense supplies of materials and instruments they were said to have. But we of China, we had to make do, we had to manage, and go on with our own resources.

Landing was a difficult matter in the almost total darkness. There was only the faint glimmer of the oil lamps in peasants' houses, and the rather darker darkness of trees. But the old plane had to get down somehow, and I put her down with the rumble of the undercarriage and the screech of the tail skid. It did not disturb Po Ku at all; he was sound asleep. I switched off the motors, got out, put the chocks behind and in front of the wheels, then returned to the plane, shut the door, and fell asleep on the floor.

Early in the morning we were both aroused by shouts outside. So we opened the door, and there was an orderly to tell us that instead of having a day off, as we thought, we had to take a General to another district where he was going to have an interview with General Chiang Kai-Shek about the war in the Nanking area. This General was a miserable fellow. He had been injured, and he was, theoretically, convalescing. We thought he was malingering. He was a very self-important man, and all the staff heartily disliked him. We had to straighten ourselves up a bit, so we made our way to our huts to get ourselves clean, to change our uniform because the General was a stickler for exactness in dress. While we were in the huts the rain came teeming down, and our gloom increased as the day became more and more overcast. Rain! We hated it as much as any Chinaman. One of the sights of China was to see the Chinese soldiers, all brave and hardy men, perhaps among the bravest soldiers in the world, but they hated rain. In China the rain came down in a teeming roar, a continuous downpour. It beat down on everything, soaking everything, soaking everyone who happened to be out in it. As we went back to our plane beneath our umbrellas we saw a

143

detachment of the Chinese army. They marched along the road by the side of the aerodrome, the road which was sodden and squelchy with water. The men looked thoroughly disheartened by the rain. They had enough hardship, enough suffering, and the rain aggravated it greatly. They marched along dispiritedly, their rifles protected by canvas bags which they had slung on their shoulders. On their backs they had sacks, criss-crossed with rope to keep it intact. Here they kept all their belongings, all their implements of war, their food, everything. On their heads they wore straw hats, and in their right hands, above their heads, they carried yellow oiled paper and bamboo umbrellas. Now it would seem amusing. But then it was perfectly ordinary to see five or six hundred soldiers marching down a road under five or six hundred umbrellas. We, too, used umbrellas to get to our plane.

We stared in amazement as we got to the side of our plane. There was a group of people there, and above their heads they were supporting a canopy of canvas, keeping the rain off the General. He beckoned us very imperiously, and said, "Which of you has the longer flying experience?" Po Ku sighed wearily, "I have, General," he said. "I have been flying for ten years, but my comrade is by far the better pilot, and has greater experience." "I am the judge of who is the best," said the General. "You will fly, and he will keep good watch over our safety." So Po Ku went to the pilot's compartment. I made my way to the tail of the plane. We tried the engines. I could watch through the little window, and I saw the General and his aides get aboard. There was much ado at the door, much ceremonial, much waving, bowing, and then an orderly closed the door of the plane, and two mechanics pulled aside the chocks at the wheels. A wave to Po Ku, and the engines were revved up. He gave me a signal on our cord and we moved off.

I did not feel at all happy about this flight. We were going to fly over the Japanese lines, and the Japanese were very alert as to who flew over their positions. Worse than that, we had three fighters—only three—which were supposed to be guarding us. We knew that they would serve as a great attraction to the Japanese, because the Japanese fighters would come up to see what was the matter, why should an old tri-motored plane like ours have fighter planes guarding it? However, as the General had stated so unmistakably, he was the senior, and he was the one who was giving the orders, and so we lumbered on. We lumbered down to the end of the field. With a swirl of dust, and a clatter of the undercarriage, the plane swung round, the three engines revved up to their limit and we rushed down the field. With a clank and a roar the old plane leapt into the air. We circled round for a time to gain height. That was not our custom, but on this occasion it was our orders. Gradually we got up to five thousand, ten thousand feet. Ten thousand was about our ceiling. We continued to circle around until the three fighters took off, and took formation above us and behind us. I felt absolutely naked, stuck up there with those three fighter planes hanging about. Every now and again I could see one slide into view from my window, and then gradually drop back out of my range of vision. It gave me no feeling of security to see them there. On the contrary, I feared every moment to see Japanese planes as well.

We droned on, and on. It seemed endless. We seemed to be suspended between heaven and earth. There were slight rocks and bumps, the plane swayed a little, and my mind wandered with the monotony of it. I thought of the war going on beneath us down on the ground. I thought of the atrocities, of the horrors, so many of which I had seen. I thought of my beloved Tibet, and how pleasant it would be if I could take even old Abie and fly off and land at the foot of the Potala in Lhasa. Suddenly there were loud bangs, the sky seemed to be filled with whirling planes, planes with the hated "bloodspot" on their wings. I could see them coming into view, and darting out again. I could see tracers and the black smoke of cannon fire. There was no point in my giving signals to Po Ku. It was self-evident that we were being heavily fired upon. Old Abie lurched and dived, and rose again. Her nose went up, and we seemed to claw at the sky. Po Ku was putting us into violent man-oeuvres, I thought, and I had my work cut out to maintain my position in the tail. Suddenly bullets came whizzing through the fabric just in front of me. At my side a wire twanged, and snapped, and the end of it scraped my face, just missing my left eye. I made myself as small as I could, and tried to force myself further back in the tail. There was a ferocious battle in progress, a battle which was now in my full view, because bullets had torn a dotted line on the fabric, and the window had gone, and many feet of material as well. I seemed to be sitting up in the clouds on a wooden framework. The battle ebbed and flowed, then there was a tremendous "CRUMP." The whole plane shook, and the nose dropped. I took one frantic look from the window. Japanese planes seemed to fill the sky. As I watched I saw a Japanese and a Chinese plane collide. There was a "BOOM" and a gout of orange-red flame followed by black smoke, and the two planes went whirling down together locked in a death embrace. The pilots spewed out, and fell whirling, hands and legs outstretched, turning over and over like wheels. It reminded me of my early kite flying days in Tibet, when the lama fell out of a kite and went whirl-ing down in much the same way, to crash upon the rocks thousands of feet below.

Once again the whole plane shuddered violently, and went wing over wing, like a falling leaf. I thought that the end had come. The nose dropped, the tail rose with such suddenness that I slid straight down the fuselage into the cabin, and into a scene of sheerest horror. The General lay dead; strewn around the cabin were the bodies of the attendants. Cannon shells had ripped through them, and

146

just about blown them to bits. All his attendants or aides were either dead or dying. The cabin was a complete shambles. I wrenched open the door of the pilot's compartment, and recoiled, feeling sick. Inside was the headless body of Po Ku, hunched over the controls. His head, or what remained of it, was spattered over the instrument panel. The windscreen was a bloody mess, blood and brains. It was so obscured that I could not see out of it. Quickly I seized Po Ku around the shoulders, and threw him aside from the seat. With utter haste I sat down, and grabbed the controls. They were thrashing about, jumping violently. They were slimy with blood, and it was with extreme difficulty that I could hold them. I pulled back on the control column to try and bring up the nose. But I could not see. I crossed my legs over the column and, shuddering, used my bare hands to scrape the brains and the blood from the windscreen, to try and make a patch so that I could see. The ground was rushing up. I saw it through the red haze of Po Ku's blood. Things were getting larger and larger. The plane was trembling, the engines were screeching. The throttles had no effect whatever upon them. The port wing engine jumped straight out. After that the starboard engine exploded. With the weight of those two gone, the nose rose slightly. I pulled back harder, and harder. The nose rose slightly more, but it was too late, much too late. The plane was too battered to answer its controls properly. I had managed to slow it somewhat, but not enough to make a satisfactory landing. The ground appeared to rise up; the wheels touched, the nose fell even more. There was a shocking scrunch, and the rending of woodwork. I felt as if the world was disintegrating around me as, together with the pilot's seat, I shot right out through the bottom of the plane into an odorous mass. There was absolutely excruciating pain in my legs, and for a time I knew no more.

It could not have been very long before I regained consciousness, because I awoke to the sound of gunfire. I looked up. Japanese planes were flying down; there were flashes of red from the gun muzzles. They were shooting at the wreckage of Old Abie, shooting to make sure there was no one in it. A little flicker of fire started at the engine, the only engine left, in the nose. It ran around toward the cabin where the fabric had been saturated with petrol. There was a sudden flare of white flame topped by black smoke. Petrol was spilling on the ground, and it looked as if there was flame pouring down because the petrol was alight. Then there was just a boom, and wreckage came raining down, and Abie was no more. Satisfied at last the Japanese planes made off.

Now I had time to look about me, and to see where I was. To my horror I found that I was in a deep drainage ditch, in a sewer. In China many of the sewers are open, and I was in one of them. The stench was simply appalling. I consoled myself with the thought that at least the position in which I had found myself had saved me from Japanese bullets, or from fire. Quickly I freed myself from the wreckage of the pilot's seat. I found that I had snapped both ankles, but with considerable effort I managed to crawl along on hands and knees, scrabbling at the crumbling earth to reach the top of the ditch, and to escape from the clinging mess of sewage.

At the top of the bank, just across from the flames which still flickered on the petrol saturated earth, I fainted again with pain and exhaustion, but heavy kicks in my ribs soon brought me back to consciousness. Japanese soldiers had been attracted to the spot by the flames, and they had found me. "Here is one who is alive," said a voice. I opened my eyes, and there was a Japanese soldier with a rifle with fixed bayonet. The bayonet was drawn back, ready for a thrust at my heart. "I had to bring him back, so that he would know he was being killed," he said to a comrade of his, and he made to thrust at me. At that moment an officer came hurrying along. "Stop!" he shouted. "Take him to the camp. We will make him tell us who were the occupants of this plane, and why they were so guarded. Take him to the camp. We will question him." So the soldier slung his rifle on his shoulder, and caught hold of me by the collar and started to drag me along. "Heavy one, this. Give me a hand," he said. One of his companions came over and caught me by an arm. Together they dragged me along, scraping off the skin of my legs at the same time as I was pulled along the stony ground. At last the officer, who apparently was doing a routine inspection, returned. With a roar of rage he shouted, "Carry him." He looked at my bleeding body, and at the trail of blood I was leaving behind, and he smacked the two guards across the face with the flat of his hand. "If he loses any more blood there will not be enough man to question, and I shall hold you responsible," he said. So for a time I was allowed to rest on the ground while one of the guards went off in search of some sort of conveyance, because I was a large man, quite bulky, and the Japanese guards were small and insignificant.

Eventually I was tossed like a sack of rubbish on to a one-wheeled barrow, and carried off to a building which the Japanese were using as a prison. Here I was just tipped off, and again dragged by the collar to a cell and left to myself. The door was slammed and locked, and the soldiers set to guard outside. After a few moments I managed to set my ankles, and put splints on. The splints were odd pieces of wood which happened to be in the cell which apparently had been used as some sort of store. To bind these splints I had to tear strips from my clothing.

For days I lay in the prison, in the solitary cell, with only rats and spiders for company. Fed once a day on a quart of water and on scraps left over from the tables of the Japanese guards, scraps which perhaps they had chewed, and found unsatisfying, and spat out. But it was the only food I had. It must have been more than a week that I was kept there, because my broken bones were getting well. Then, after

149

midnight, the door was roughly flung open, and Japanese guards entered noisily. I was dragged to my feet. They had to support me because my ankles were still not strong enough to take my weight. Then an officer came in and smacked me across the face. "Your name?" he said. "I am an officer of the Chinese forces, and I am a prisoner-of-war. That is all I have to say," I replied. "MEN do not allow themselves to be taken prisoners. Prisoners are scum without rights. You will answer me," said the officer. But I made no reply. So they knocked me about the head with the flat of their swords, they punched me, kicked me, and spat at me. As I still did not answer they burned me about the face and body with lighted cigarettes, and put lighted matches between my fingers. My training had not been in vain. I said nothing, they could not make me talk. I just kept silent and put my mind to other thoughts, knowing that that was the best way of doing things. Eventually a guard brought a rifle butt down across my back, knocking the wind out of me, and almost stunning me with the violence of the blow. The officer walked across to me, spat in my face, gave me a hard kick, and said, "We shall be back, you will speak then." I had collapsed on the floor, so I stayed there, there was no other place to rest. I tried to recover my strength somewhat. That night there was no further disturbance, nor did I see anyone the next day, nor the day after that, nor the day after that. For three days and four nights I was kept with no food, no water, and without seeing anyone at all. Kept in suspense, wondering what would happen next.

On the fourth day an officer came again, a different one, and said that they were going to look after me, that they were going to treat me well, but that I in return must tell them all that I knew about the Chinese, and about the Chinese forces and Chiang Kai-Shek. They said that they had found out who I was, that I was a high noble from Tibet, and they wanted Tibet to be friendly with them. I thought to myself, "Well they are certainly showing a peculiar form of friendship." The officer just made a bow, turned, and left.

For a week I was reasonably well treated, given two meals a day, and water, and that was all. Not enough water, and not enough food, but at least they left me alone. But then three of them came together, and said that they were going to question me, and I was going to answer their questions. They brought a Japanese doctor in with them who examined me, and said that I was in bad shape, but I was well enough to be questioned. He looked at my ankles, and said that it was a marvel that I could possibly walk after. Then they bowed ceremoniously to me, and ceremoniously to each other, and trooped out like a gang of schoolboys. Once again the cell door clanged behind them, and I knew that later on that day I was going to face interrogation once again. I composed my mind, and determined that no matter what they did I would not betray the Chinese.

CHAPTER EIGHT

When the World was Very Young

IN the early hours of next morning, long before the first streaks of dawn appeared in the sky, the cell door was flung open violently, to recoil against the stone wall with a clang. Guards rushed in, I was dragged to my feet, and shaken roughly by three or four men. Then handcuffs were put upon me, and I was marched off to a room which seemed to be a long, long way away. The guards kept prodding me with their rifle butts, not gently either. Every time they did this, which was all too frequent, they yelled,

151

"Answer all questions promptly, you enemy of peace. Answer truthfully or terrible things will be done to you. You are an enemy of peace. We will get the truth from you."

Eventually we reached the Interrogation Room. Here there were a group of officers sitting in a semicircle, looking fierce, or trying to look fierce. Actually, to me, they seemed to be a gang of schoolboys who were out for a sadistic treat. They all bowed ceremoniously as I was brought in. Then a senior officer, a colonel, exhorted me to tell the truth. He assured me that the Japanese people were friendly, and peace-loving. But I, he said, was an enemy of the Japanese people because I was trying to resist their peaceful penetration into China. China, he told me, should have been a colony of the Japanese, because China was without culture! He continued, "We Japanese are true friends of peace. You must tell us all. Tell us of the Chinese movements, and of their strength, and of your talks with Chiang Kai-Shek, so that we may crush the rebellion of China without loss of our own soldiers." I said, "I am a prisoner-of-war, and demand to be treated as such. I have nothing more to say." He said, "We have to see that all men live in peace under the Emperor. We are going to have an expanded Japanese Empire. You will tell the truth." They were not at all gentle in their methods of questioning. They wanted information, and they didn't mind what they did to get that information. I refused to say anything, so they knocked me down with rifle butts—rifle butts dashed brutally against my chest or back, or at my knees. Then I was pulled to my feet again by guards so that I could be knocked down again. After many, many hours, during which time I was burned with cigarette ends, they decided that stronger measures were called for. I was bound hand and foot, and dragged off again to an underground cell. Here I was kept bound hand and foot for several days. The Japanese method of tying prisoners led to excruciating pain. My wrists were tied behind me with my hands point-

152

ing to the back of my neck. Then my ankles were tied to my wrists, and legs were folded at the knees, so that the soles of the feet also faced the back of the neck. Then a rope was passed from my left ankle and wrist around my neck, and down to the right ankle and wrist. So that if I tried to ease my position at all I half strangled myself. It was indeed a painful process, being kept like a strong bow. Every so often a guard would come in and kick me just to see what happened.

For several days I was kept like that, being unbound for half-an-hour a day only; for several days they kept me like that, and they kept coming and asking for information. I made no sound or response other than to say, "I am an officer of the Chinese forces, a non-combatant officer. I am a doctor and a prisoner-of-war. I have nothing more to say." Eventually they got tired of asking me questions, so they brought in a hose, and they poured strongly peppered water into my nostrils. I felt as if my whole brain was on fire. It felt as if devils were stoking the flames within me. But I did not speak, and they kept on mixing a stronger solution of pepper and water, adding mustard to it. The pain was quite considerable. Eventually bright blood came out of my mouth. The pepper had burned out the linings of my nostrils. I had managed to survive this for ten days, and I supposed it occurred to them that that method would not make me talk, so, at sight of the bright red blood, they went away.

Two or three days later they came for me again, and carried me to the Interrogation Room. I had to be carried because this time I could not walk in spite of my efforts, in spite of being bludgeoned with gun butts and pricked with bayonets. My hands and legs had been bound for so long that I just could not use them at all. Inside the Interrogation Room I was just dropped to the floor, and the guards —four of them—who had been carrying me stood to attention before the officers who were sitting in a semi-circle.

This time they had before them many strange implements which I, from my studies, knew to be instruments of torture. "You will tell us the truth now, and cease to waste our time," said the colonel. "I have told you the truth. I am an officer of the Chinese forces." That was all I said in reply.

The Japanese went red in the face with anger, and at a command I was strapped to a board, with my arms outstretched as if I was on a cross. Long slivers of bamboo were inserted beneath my nails right down to the little finger joints, then the slivers were rotated. It really was painful, but it still brought no response. So the guards quickly pulled out the slivers, and then slowly, one by one, my nails were split off backwards.

The pain was truly devilish. It was worse when the Japanese dropped salt water onto the bleeding finger ends. I knew that I must not talk and betray my comrades, and so I called to mind the advice of my Guide, the Lama Mingyar Dondup. "Do not concentrate on the seat of the pain, Lobsang, for if you do you focus all your energies on that spot, and then the pain cannot be borne. Instead think of something else. Control your mind, and think of something else, because if you do that you will still have the pain and the after-effects of pain, but you will be able to bear it. It will seem as something in the background." So to keep my sanity, and to avoid giving names and information I put my mind to other things. I thought of the past, of my home in Tibet, and of my Guide. I thought of the beginnings of things as we knew them in Tibet.

Beneath the Potala were hidden mysterious tunnels, tunnels which may hold the key to the history of the world. These interested me, they fascinated me, and it may be of interest to recall once again what I saw and learned there, for it is knowledge apparently not possessed by Western peoples.

I remembered how at the time I was a very young monk

in training. The Inmost One, the Dalai Lama, had been making use of my services at the Potala as a clairvoyant, and He had been well pleased with me and as a reward had given me the run of the place. My Guide, the Lama Mingyar Dondup, sent for me one day. "Lobsang, I have been thinking a lot about your evolution, and I have come to the conclusion that you are now of such an age and have attained such a state of development that you can study with me the writings in the hidden caves. Come!"

He rose to his feet, and with me at his side we went out of his room, down the corridor, down many, many steps, past groups of monks working at their daily tasks, attending to the domestic economy of the Potala. Eventually, far down in the gloom of the mountain, we came to a little room branching off to the right of the corridor. Little light came through the windows here. Outside the ceremonial prayer flags flapped in the breeze. "We will enter here, Lobsang, and we will take lamps so that we may explore those regions to which only very few lamas have access." In the little room we took lamps from the shelves, and filled them. Then, as a precaution, we each took a spare. Our main lamps were lit, and we walked out, and down the corridor, my Guide ahead of me showing me the way. Down we went, down the corridor, ever down. At long last we came to a room at the end. It seemed to be the end of a journey to me. It appeared to be a storeroom. Strange figures were about, images, sacred objects, and foreign gods, gifts from all the world over. Here was where the Dalai Lama kept his overflow of gifts, those for which He had no immediate use.

I looked about me with intense curiosity. There was no sense in being here so far as I could see. I thought we were going exploring, and this was just a storage room. "Illustrious Master," I said, "surely we have mistaken our path in coming here?" The lama looked at me, and smiled benevolently. "Lobsang, Lobsang, do you think I would lose my way?" He smiled as he turned away from me, and walked to a far wall. For a moment he looked about him, and then did something. As far as I could see he was fiddling about with some pattern on the wall, some plaster protuberance apparently fabricated by some long-dead hand. Eventually there was a rumble as of falling stones, and I spun around in alarm, thinking that perhaps the ceiling was caving in or the floor was collapsing. My Guide laughed. "Oh, no, Lobsang, we are quite safe, quite safe. This is where we continue our journey. This is where we step into another world. A world that few have seen. Follow me."

I looked in awe. The section of the wall had slid aside revealing a dark hole. I could see a dusty path going from the room into the hole, and disappearing into the stygian gloom. The sight rooted me to the spot in astonishment. "But Master!" I exclaimed, "there was no sign of a door at all there. How did it happen so?" My Guide laughed at me, and said, "This is an entry which was made centuries ago. The secret of it has been well preserved. Unless one knows one cannot open this door, and no matter how thoroughly one searches there is no sign of a joint or of a crack. But come, Lobsang, we are not discussing building procedure. We are wasting time. You will see this place often." With that he turned and led the way into the hole, into the mysterious tunnel reaching far ahead. I followed with considerable trepidation. He allowed me to go past him, then he turned and again manipulated something. Again came the ominous rumbling and creaking and grating, and a whole panel of the living rock slid before my startled eyes and covered the hole. We were now in darkness, lit only by the flickering glimmer of the golden-flamed butter lamps which we carried. My Guide passed me, and marched on. His footsteps, muffled though they were, echoed curiously from the rock sides, echoed, and re-echoed. He walked on without speaking. We seemed to cover more than a mile, then suddenly without warning, so suddenly that I bumped into him with an exclamation of astonishment, the lama ahead of me stopped. "Here we replenish our lamps, Lobsang, and put in bigger wicks. We shall need light now. Do as I do, and then we will continue our journey."

Now we had a somewhat brighter flame to light our way, and we continued for a long, long way, for so long that I was getting tired and fidgety. Then I noticed that the passageway was getting wider and higher. It seemed as if we were walking along the narrow end of a funnel, approaching the wider end. We rounded a corridor and I shouted in amazement. I saw before me a vast cavern. From the roof and sides came innumerable pinpoints of golden light, light reflected from our butter lamps. The cavern appeared to be immense. Our feeble illumination only emphasised the immensity and the darkness of it.

My Guide went to a crevice at the left-side of the path, and with a screech dragged out what appeared to be a large metal cylinder. It seemed to be half as high as a man, and certainly as wide as a man at the thickest part. It was round, and there was a device at the top which I did not understand. It seemed to be a small, white net. The Lama Mingyar Dondup fiddled about with the thing, and then touched the top of it with his butter lamp. Immediately there was a bright yellow-white flame which enabled me to see clearly. There was a faint hissing from the light, as if it was being forced out under pressure. My Guide extinguished our little lamps then. "We shall have plenty of light with this, Lobsang, we will take it with us. I want you to learn some of the history from aeons of long ago." He moved ahead, pulling this great bright light, this flaming canister, on a thing like a little sledge. It moved easily. We walked on down the path once again, ever down, until I thought that we must be right down in the bowels of the earth. Eventually he stopped. Before me was a black wall, shot with a great panel of gold, and on the gold were engravings, hundreds, thousands of them. I looked at them, then I looked away to the other side. I could see the black shimmer of water, as if before me was a great lake.

"Lobsang, pay attention to me. You will know about that later. I want to tell you a little of the origin of Tibet, an origin which in later years you will be able to verify for yourself when you go upon an expedition which I am even now planning," he said. "When you go away from our land you will find those who know us not who will say that Tibetans are illiterate savages who worship devils and indulge in unmentionable rites. But Lobsang, we have a culture far older than any in the West, we have records carefully hidden and preserved going back through the ages..."

He went across to the inscriptions and pointed out various figures, various symbols. I saw drawings of people, of animals—animals such as we know not now—and then he pointed out a map of the sky, but a map which even I knew was not of the present day because the stars it showed were different and in the wrong places. The lama paused, and turned to me. "I understand this, Lobsang, I was taught this language. Now I will read it to you, read you this age-old story, and then in the days to come I and others will teach you this secret language so that you can come here and make your own notes, keep your own records, and draw your own conclusions. It will mean study, study, study. You will have to come and explore these caverns for there are many of them and they extend for miles beneath us."

For a moment he stood looking at the inscriptions. Then he read to me part of the past. Much of what he said then, and very much more of what I studied later, simply cannot be given in a book such as this. The average reader would not believe, and if he did and he knew some of the secrets, then he might do as others have done in the past; use the

158

devices which I have seen for self-gain, to obtain mastery over others, and to destroy others as nations are now threatening to destroy each other with the atom bomb. The atom bomb is not a new discovery. It was discovered thousands of years ago, and it brought disaster to the earth then as it will do now if man is not stopped in his folly.

In every religion of the world, in every history of every tribe and nation, there is the story of the Flood, of a catastrophe in which peoples were drowned, in which lands sank and land rose, and the earth was in turmoil. That is in the history of the Incas, the Egyptians, the Christians— everyone. That, so we know, was caused by a bomb; but let me tell you how it happened, according to the inscriptions.

My Guide seated himself in the lotus position, facing the inscriptions on the rock, with the brilliant light at his back shining with a golden glare upon those age-old engravings. He motioned for me to be seated also. I took my place by his side, so that I could see the features to which he pointed. When I had settled myself he started to talk, and this is what he told me.

"In the days of long, long ago earth was a very different place. It revolved much nearer the sun, and in the opposite direction, and there was another planet nearby, a twin of the earth. Days were shorter, and so man seemed to have a longer life. Man seemed to live for hundreds of years. The climate was hotter, and flora was both tropical and luxurious. Fauna grew to huge size and in many diverse forms. The force of gravity was much less than it is at present because of the different rate of rotation of the earth, and man was perhaps twice as large as he is now, but even so he was a pigmy compared to another race who lived with him. For upon the earth lived those of a different system who were super-intellectuals. They supervised the earth, and taught men much. Man then was as a colony, as a class that is being taught by a kindly teacher. These

159

huge giants taught him much. Often they would get in strange craft of gleaming metal and would sweep across the sky. Man, poor ignorant man, still upon the threshold of dawning reason, could not understand it at all, for his intellect was hardly greater than that of the apes.

"For countless ages life on earth followed a placid path. There was peace and harmony between all creatures. Men could converse without speech, by telepathy. They used speech only for local conversations. Then the super-intellectuals, who were so much larger than man, quarrelled. Dissentient forces rose up among them. They could not agree on certain issues just as races now cannot agree. One group went off to another part of the world, and tried to rule. There was strife. Some of the super-men killed each other, and they waged fierce wars, and brought much destruction to each other. Man, eager to learn, learned the arts of war; man learned to kill. So the earth which before had been a peaceful place became a troubled spot. For some time, for some years, the super-men worked in secret, one half of them against the other half. One day there was a tremendous explosion, and the whole earth seemed to shake and veer in its course. Lurid flames shot across the sky, and the earth was wreathed in smoke. Eventually the uproar died down, but after many months strange signs were seen in the sky, signs that filled the people of earth with terror. A planet was approaching, and rapidly growing bigger, and bigger. It was obvious that it was going to strike the earth. Great tides arose, and the winds with it, and the days and nights were filled with a howling tempestuous fury. A planet appeared to fill the whole sky until at last it seemed that it must crash straight onto the earth. As the planet got closer, and closer, immense tidal waves arose, and drowned whole tracts of land. Earthquakes shivered the surface of the globe, and continents were swallowed in the twinkling of an eye. The race of supermen forgot their quarrels; they hastened to their gleaming machines, and rose up into the sky, and sped away from the trouble besetting the earth. But on the earth itself earthquakes continued; mountains rose up, and the sea-bed rose with them; lands sank and were inundated with water; people of that time fled in terror, crazed with fear at what they thought was the end of the world, and all the time the winds grew fiercer, and the uproar and the clamour harder to bear, uproar and clamour which seemed to shatter the nerves and drive men to frenzy.

"The invading planet grew closer and larger, until at last it approached to within a certain distance and there was a tremendous crash, and a vivid electric spark shot from it. The skies flamed with continuous discharges, and soot-black clouds formed and turned the days into a continuous night of fearful terror. It seemed that the sun itself stood still with horror at the calamity, for, according to the records, for many, many days the red ball of the sun stood still, blood-red with great tongues of flame shooting from it. Then eventually the black clouds closed, and all was night. The winds grew cold, then hot; thousands died with the change of temperature, and the change again. Food of the Gods, which some called manna, fell from the sky. Without it the people of the earth, and the animals of the world, would have starved through the destruction of the crops, through the deprivation of all other food.

"Men and women wandered from place to place looking for shelter, looking for anywhere where they could rest their weary bodies wracked by the storm, tortured by the turmoil; praying for quiet, hoping to be saved. But the earth shook and shivered, the rains poured down, and all the time from the outer space came the splashes and discharges of electricity. With the passage of time, as the heavy black clouds rolled away, the sun was seen to be coming smaller, and smaller. It seemed to be receding, and the people of the world cried out in fear. They thought the Sun God, the Giver of Life, was running away from them. But stranger still the sun now moved across the sky from east to west, instead of from west to east as before.

"Man had lost all track of time. With the obscuring of the sun there was no method with which they could tell its passage; not even the wisest men knew how long ago these events had taken place. Another strange thing was seen in the sky; a world, quite a large world, yellow, gibbous, which seemed as if it too was going to fall upon the earth. This which we now know as the moon appeared at this time as a relic from the collision of the two planets. Later races were to find a great depression in the earth, in Siberia, where perhaps the surface of the earth had been damaged by the close proximity of another world, or even a spot from whence the moon had been wrenched.

"Before the collision there had been cities and tall buildings housing much knowledge of the Greater Race. They had been toppled in the turmoil, and they were just mounds of rubble, concealing all that hidden knowledge. The wise men of the tribes knew that within those mounds were canisters containing specimens and books of engraved metal. They knew that all the knowledge in the world reposed within those piles of rubbish, and so they set to work to dig, and dig, to see what could be saved in the records, so that they could increase their own power by making use of the knowledge of the Greater Race.

"Throughout the years to come the days became longer, and longer, until they were almost twice as long as before the calamity, and then the earth settled in its new orbit, accompanied by its moon, the moon, a product of a collision. But still the earth shook and rumbled, and mountains rose and spewed out flames and rocks, and destruction. Great rivers of lava rushed down the mountain sides without warning, destroying all that lay in their path, but often enclosing monuments and sources of knowledge, for the hard metal upon which many of the records had been written was not melted by the lava, but merely protected by

162

it, preserved in a casing of stone, porous stone which in the course of time eroded away, so that the records contained within would be revealed and would fall into the hands of those who would make use of them. But that was not for a long time yet. Gradually, as the earth became more settled in its new orbit, cold crept upon the world, and animals died or moved to the warmer areas. The mammoth and the brontosaurus died for they could not adapt to the new ways of life. Ice fell from the sky, and the winds grew bitter. Now there were many clouds, whereas before there had been almost none. The world was a very different place; the sea had tides; before they had been placid lakes, unruffled except by the passing breeze. Now great waves lashed up at the sky, and for years the tides were immense and threatened to engulf the land and drown the people. The heavens looked different too. At night strange stars were seen in place of the familiar ones, and the moon was very close. New religions sprouted as the priests of that time tried to maintain their power and account for the happenings. They forgot much about the Greater Race, they thought only of their own power, of their own importance. But—they could not say how this occurred, or how that happened. They put it down to the wrath of God, and taught that all man was born in sin.

"With the passage of time, with the earth settled in its new orbit, and as the weather became more tranquil, people grew smaller and shorter. The centuries rolled by, and lands became more stable. Many races appeared as if experimentally, struggled, failed, and disappeared, to be replaced by others. At last a stronger type evolved, and civilization began anew, civilization which carried from its earliest days a racial memory of some dire calamity, and some of the stronger intellects made search to find out what had really happened. By now the wind and the rain had done their work. The old records were beginning to appear from the crumbling lava stone, and the higher intellect of humans

163

now upon the earth were able to gather these and place them before their wise men, who at long last, with much struggle, were able to decipher some of the writings. As a little of the records became legible, and as the scientists of the day began to understand them, they set about on frantic searches for other records with which to piece together the complete instructions, and to bridge the gaps. Great excavations were undertaken, and much of interest came to light. Then indeed the new civilization sprouted. Towns and cities were built, and science started its rush to destroy. The emphasis always on destruction, upon gaining power for little groups. It was completely overlooked that man could live in peace, and that the lack of peace had caused the calamity before.

"For many centuries science held sway. The priests set up as scientists, and they outlawed all those scientists who were not also priests. They increased their power; they worshipped science, they did all they could to keep power in their own hands, and to crush the ordinary man and to stop him from thinking. They set themselves up as Gods; no work could be done without the sanction of the priests. What the priests wanted they took: without hindrance, without opposition, and all the time they were increasing their power until upon earth they were absolutely omnipotent, forgetting that for humans absolute power corrupts.

"Great craft sailed through the air without wings, without sound, sailed through the air, or hovered motionless as not even the birds could hover. The scientists had discovered the secret of mastering gravity, and anti-gravity, and harnessing it to their power. Immense blocks of stone were manoeuvred into position where wanted by one man and a very small device which could be held in the palm of one hand. No work was too hard, because man merely manipulated his machines without effort to himself. Huge engines clattered across the surface of the earth, but nothing moved upon the surface of the sea except for pleasure, because travel by sea was too slow except for those who wanted the enjoyment of the combination of wind and the waves. Everything travelled by air, or for shorter journeys across the earth. People moved out to different lands, and set up colonies. But now they had lost their telepathic power through the calamity of the collision. Now they no longer spoke a common language; the dialects became more and more acute, until in the end they were completely different, and to each other incomprehensible, languages.

"With the lack of communication, and the failure to understand each other, and each other's view points, races quarrelled, and began wars. Fearsome weapons were invented. Battles raged everywhere. Men and women were becoming maimed, and the terrible rays which were being produced were making many mutations in the human race. Years rolled by, and the struggle became more intense, and the carnage more terrible. Inventors everywhere, spurred on by their rulers, strove to produce more deadly weapons. Scientists worked to devise even more ghastly devices of offence. Disease germs were bred, and dropped upon the enemy from high-flying aircraft. Bombs wrecked the sewage systems, so that disease and plagues raged through the earth blighting people, animals, and plants. The earth was set on destruction.

"In a remote district far from all the strife a group of far-seeing priests who had not been contaminated by the search for power, took thin plates of gold, and engraved upon them the history of their times, engraved upon them maps of the heavens and of the lands. Upon them they revealed the innermost secrets of their science, and gave grave warnings of the dangers which would befall those who misused this knowledge. Years passed during which time these plates were prepared, and then, with specimens of the actual weapons, tools, books, and all useful things, they were concealed in stone and were hidden in various places so that those who came after them would know of the past, and would, it was hoped, profit from it. For these priests knew of the course of humanity; they knew what was to happen, and as predicted the expected did happen. A fresh weapon was made, and tried. A fantastic cloud swirled up into the stratosphere, and the earth shook, and reeled again, and seemed to rock on its axis. Immense walls of water surged over the land, and swept away many of the races of man. Once again mountains sank beneath the seas, and others rose up to take their place. Some men, women, and animals, who had been warned by these priests, were saved by being afloat in ships, afloat and sealed against the poisonous gases and germs which ravaged the earth. Other men and women were carried high into the air as the lands upon which they dwelt rose up; others, not so fortunate, were carried down, perhaps beneath the water, or perhaps down as the mountains closed over their heads.

"Flood and flames and lethal rays killed people in millions, and very few people only were left on earth now, isolated from each other by vagaries of the catastrophe. These were half-crazed by the disaster, shaken out of their senses by the tremendous noise and commotion. For many years they hid in caves and in thick forests. They forgot all the culture, and they went back to the wild stages, as in the earliest days of mankind, covering themselves with skin and with the juice of berries, and carrying clubs studded with flint in their hands.

"Eventually new tribes were formed, and they wandered over the new face of the world. Some settled in what is now Egypt, others in China, but those of the pleasant low-lying seaside resort, which had been much favoured by the super-race, suddenly found themselves many thousands of feet above the sea, ringed by the eternal mountains, and with the land fast cooling. Thousands died in the bitter, rarefied air. Others who survived became the founders of the modern, hardy Tibetan of the land which is now Tibet. That had been the place in which the group of far-seeing priests had taken their thin plates of gold, and engraved upon them all their secrets. Those plates, and all the specimens of their arts and crafts, had been hidden deep in a cavern in a mountain to become accessible to a later race of priests. Others were hidden in a great city which is now in the Chang Tang Highlands of Tibet.

"All culture was not quite extinct, however, although mankind was back in the savage state, in the Black Ages. But there were isolated spots throughout the earth's surface where little groups of men and women struggled on to keep knowledge alive, to keep alight the flickering flame of human intellect, a little group struggling on blindly in the stygian darkness of savagery. Throughout the centuries which followed there were many states of religion, many attempts to find the truth of what had happened, and all the time hidden away in Tibet in deep caves was knowledge. Engraved upon plates of imperishable gold, permanent, uncorruptible, waiting for those who could find them, and decipher them.

"Gradually man developed once again. The gloom of ignorance began to dissipate. Savagery turned to semi-civilisation. There was actually progress of a sort. Again cities were built, and machines flew in the sky. Once more the mountains were no bar, man travelled throughout the world, across the seas, and over the land. As before, with the increase of knowledge and power, they became arrogant, and oppressed weaker peoples. There was unrest, hatred, persecution, and secret research. The stronger people oppressed the weak. The weaker peoples developed machines, and there were wars, wars again lasting years. Ever there were fresh and more terrible weapons being produced. Each side sought to find the most terrible weapons of all, and all the time in caves in Tibet knowledge was lying. All the time in the Chang Tang Highlands a great city lay desolate, unguarded, containing the most precious knowledge in the world, waiting for those who would enter, and see, lying, just waiting . . ."

167

Lying. I was lying on my back in an underground cell in a prison, looking up through a red haze. Blood was pouring from my nose, from my mouth, from the ends of my fingers, and toes. I ached all over. I felt as if I were immersed in a bath of flame. Dimly I heard a Japanese voice say, "You've gone too far this time. He cannot live. He cannot possibly live." But I did live. I determined that I would live on, and show the Japanese how a man of Tibet conducted himself. I would show them not even their most devilish tortures would make a Tibetan speak.

My nose was broken, was squashed flat against my face by an angry bang from a rifle butt. My mouth was gashed, my jaw bones were broken, my teeth kicked out. But not all the tortures of the Japanese could make me talk. After a time they gave up the attempt, for even the Japanese could realise the futility of trying to make a man talk when he would not. After many weeks I was set to work dealing with the bodies of others who had not survived. The Japanese thought that by giving me such a job they would eventually break my nerve, and perhaps then I would talk. Piling up bodies in the heat of the sun, bodies stinking, bloated, and discoloured, was not pleasant. Bodies would swell up, and burst like pricked balloons. One day I saw a man fall dead. I knew he was dead because I examined him myself, but the guards took no notice; he was just picked up by two men, and swung and tossed on to the pile of dead bodies, and left, left so that the hot sun and the rats could do the work of scavenging. But it did not matter if a man was dead or not, because if a man was too ill to work he was either bayoneted on the spot and tossed on to the dead pile, or he was tossed on while he was still alive.

I decided that I too would "die," and would be placed with the other bodies. During the hours of darkness I would escape. So I made my few plans, and for the next three or four days I carefully watched the Japanese and their procedure, and decided on how I would act. For a day or so

I staggered, and acted as if I were weaker than I really was. On the day on which I planned to "die" I staggered as I walked, staggered as I attended roll-call at the first light of dawn. Throughout the morning I showed every sign of utter weariness, and then, just after noon, I let myself collapse. It was not difficult, not really acting, I could have collapsed with weariness at any time. The tortures I had undergone had weakened me considerably. The poor food I had, had weakened me even more, and I was indeed deadly tired. This time I did collapse, and actually fell asleep through tiredness. I felt my body being crudely lifted and swung, and tossed up. The impact as I landed on the pile of creaking dead bodies awakened me. I felt the pile sway a little and then settle down. The shock of that landing made me open my eyes; a guard was looking half-heartedly in my direction, so I opened my eyes still more as a dead man's eyes go, and he looked away, he was too used to seeing dead bodies, one more was of no interest to him. I kept very still, very still indeed, thinking of the past again, and planning for the future. I kept still in spite of other bodies being thrown up around me, on top of me.

The day seemed to last years. I thought the light would never fade. But at long last it did, the first signs of night were coming. The stench about me was almost unbearable, the stench of long-dead bodies. Beneath me I could hear the rustling and squeaks of rats going about their gruesome work, eating the bodies. Every now and then the pile would sag as one of the bottom bodies collapsed under the weight of all those above. The pile would sag and sway, and I hoped that it would not topple over, as so often it did, for then the bodies would have to be piled again, and who knows—this time I might be found to be alive, or even worse, find myself at the bottom of the pile, when my plight would be hopeless.

At last the prisoners working around were marched in to their huts. The guards patrolled the top of the wall, and there was the chill of the night air. Slowly, oh, so slowly, the light began to fade. One by one little yellow lights appeared in windows, in the guardrooms. So slowly as to be almost imperceptible, night came.

For a long, long time I lay still in that stinking bed of dead bodies. Lay still watching as best I could. Then, when the guards were at the far end of their beat, I gingerly pushed aside a body from above me, and pushed away one at my side. It tumbled, and went over the side of the pile, and fell upon the ground with a crunch. I held my breath with dismay; I thought that surely now guards would come running, and I would be found. It was death indeed to move outside in the darkness, because searchlights would come on, and any unfortunate found by the Japanese would be bayoneted to death, or disembowelled perhaps, or hung over a slow fire, or any devilish death which the distorted Japanese ingenuity could devise, and all this would be in front of a sickened group of prisoners, to teach them that it was not policy to try to escape from the Sons of Heaven.

Nothing moved. The Japanese were too used, apparently, to the creakings and fallings from the dead pile. I moved experimentally. The whole pile of bodies creaked and shook. I moved a foot at a time, and eventually crept over the edge of the pile, and let myself down, grabbing bodies so that I could climb down ten or twelve feet, because I was too weak to jump and risk a sprain or a broken bone. The slight noises that I made did not attract attention. The Japanese had no idea at all that anyone would hide in such a gruesome place. Upon the ground I moved stealthily and slowly to the shadow of the trees near the wall of the prison camp. For some time I waited. Above my head the guards came together. There was a muttered talk, and the flare of a match as a cigarette was lighted. Then the guards parted, one going off up the wall, and the other down, each with a cigarette hidden in his cupped hands, each of them more or less blinded for the time being by the glare of that match in the darkness. I took advantage of that. Quietly and slowly I managed to climb over the wall. This was a camp which had been set up temporarily, and the Japanese had not got around to electrifying their fences. I climbed over, and stealthily made my way into the darkness. All that night I lay along the branch of a tree, almost in sight of the camp. I reasoned that if I had been missed, if I had been seen, the Japanese would rush by, they would not think that a prisoner would stay so close to them.

The whole of the next day I stayed where I was, I was too weak, and ill, to move. Then at the end of the day, as the darkness again fell, I slithered down the trunk of the tree, and made my way on through territory which I knew well.

I knew that an old, old Chinese lived nearby. I had brought much help to his wife before she died, and to his house I made my way in the darkness. I tapped gently at his door. There was an air of tenseness, an air of fright. Eventually I whispered who I was. Stealthy movements inside, and then gently and silently the door was opened a few inches, and the old face looked out. "Ah," he said, "come in quickly." He opened the door wider, and I crept in beneath his outstretched arm. He put up his shutters, and lit a light, and gasped with horror as he saw me. My left eye was badly damaged. My nose was flattened against my face. My mouth was cut and gashed, and the ends drooped down. He heated water; and washed my hurts, and gave me food. That night and the next day I rested in his hut. He went out, and made arrangements whereby I should be conveyed to the Chinese lines. For several days I had to remain in that hut in the Japanese held territory, for several days while fever raged, and where I nearly died.

After perhaps ten days I was sufficiently recovered to be able to get up, and walk out, and make my way along a well planned route to the Chinese headquarters near

Shanghai. They looked at me in horror as I went in with my squashed and battered face, and for more than a month I was in hospital while they took bone from a leg to rebuild my nose. Then I was sent off again to Chungking to recuperate before returning as an active medical officer to the Chinese medical forces. Chungking! I thought I would be glad to see it after all my adventures, after all that I had gone through. Chungking! And so I set off with a friend who also was going there to recuperate from illnesses caused in the war.

CHAPTER NINE

Prisoner of the Japanese

WE were amazed at the difference in Chungking. This was no longer the Chungking that we knew. New buildings— new fronts to old buildings—shops of all types springing up everywhere. Chungking! The place was absolutely crowded! People had been pouring in from Shanghai, from all the coastal towns. Businessmen, with their living gone on the coast, had come far inland to Chungking, to start all over again, perhaps with a few pitiful remnants saved from the grasping Japanese. But more often starting again from nothing.

Universities had found buildings in Chungking, or had built their own temporary buildings, ramshackle sheds most of them. But here was the seat of culture of China. No matter what the buildings were like, the brains were there, some of the best brains in the whole world.

We made our way to the temple at which we had stayed previously; it was like coming home. Here, in the calm of the temple, with the incense waving in clouds above our heads, we felt that we had come to peace, we felt that the Sacred Images were gazing benignly upon us in favour of our efforts, and perhaps even a little sympathetic at the harsh treatment which we had undergone. Yes, we were home at peace, recovering from our hurts, before going out into the fierce savage world to endure fresh and worse torments. The temple bells chimed, the trumpets were sounded. It was time again for the familiar, well beloved service. We took our places with hearts full of joy at being back.

That night we were late in retiring because there was so much to discuss, so much to tell, so much to hear as well, because Chungking had been having a hard time with the bombs dropping. But we were from "the great outside," as they called it in the temple, and our throats were parched before we were allowed to roll again in our blankets and sleep in the old familiar place upon the ground near the temple precincts. At last sleep overtook us.

In the morning I had to go to the hospital at which I had previously been student, house surgeon, and then medical officer. This time I was going as a patient. It was a novel experience indeed to be a patient at this hospital. My nose, though, was giving trouble; it had turned septic, and so there was nothing for it but to have it opened and scraped. This was quite a painful process. We had no anaesthetics. The Burman Road had been closed. All our supplies had been stopped. There was nothing for it but to endure, as pleasantly as I could, that which could not be avoided. But so soon as the operation was over I returned to the temple, because beds in Chungking hospital were very scarce. Wounded were pouring in, and only the most urgent cases, only those who could not walk at all, were allowed to remain in the hospital. Day after day I made the journey down the little path, along the highroad, to Chungking. At long last, after two or three weeks, the Dean of the Surgical Faculty called me into his office, and said, "Well, Lobsang,

173

my friend, we shall not have to engage thirty-two coolies for you after all. We thought we should, you know, it has been touch and go!"

Funerals in China are taken very, very seriously indeed. It was considered of the utmost importance to have the correct number of bearers according to one's social status. To me it all seemed silly, as I well knew when the spirit had left the body it did not matter at all what happened to the body. We of Tibet made no fuss about our discarded bodies; we just had them collected by the Body Breakers, who broke them up and fed the bits to the birds. Not so in China. Here that would be almost akin to condemning one to eternal torment! Here one had to have a coffin borne by thirty-two coolies if it was a first class funeral. The second class funeral, though, had just half that number of bearers, sixteen of them, as if it took sixteen men to carry one coffin! The third class funeral—this was about the average —had eight coolies bearing the lacquered wooden coffin. But the fourth class, which was just the ordinary working class, had four coolies. Of course the coffin here would be quite a light affair, quite cheap. Lower than fourth class had no coolies at all to carry. The coffins were just trundled along in any sort of conveyance. And of course there were not only coolies to be considered; there were the official mourners, those who wept and wailed, and made it their life's work to attend on the departure of the dead.

Funerals? Death? It is strange how odd incidents stay in one's mind! One in particular has stayed in mine ever since. It occurred near Chungking. It may be of interest to relate it here, to give a little picture of war—and death.

It was the day of the mid-autumn festival of "The Fifteenth Day of the Eighth Month" when the autumn moon was at the full. In China this is an auspicious occasion. It is the time when families try their utmost to come together for a banquet at the ending of the day. "Moon-cakes" are eaten to celebrate the harvest moon; they are eaten as a sort of sacrifice as a sort of token that they hope the next year will be a happier one.

My friend Huang the Chinese monk was also staying at the temple. He too had been wounded, and on this particular day we were walking from Chiaoting Village to Chungking. The village is a suburb perched high on the steep sides of the Yangtse. Here lived the wealthier people, those who could afford the best. Below us through occasional gaps in the trees as we walked we could see the river and the boats upon it. Nearer in the terraced gardens blue-clad men and women worked, bent over at their eternal weeding and hoeing. The morning was beautiful. It was warm and sunny, the type of day when one feels glad to be alive, the type of day when everything seems bright and cheerful. Thoughts of war were far removed from our minds as we strolled along, stopping every so often to look through the trees and admire the view. Close to us in a nearby thicket a bird was singing, welcoming the day. We walked on and breasted the hill. "Stop a minute, Lobsang. I'm winded," said Huang. So we sat on a boulder in the shadow of the trees. It was pleasant there with the beautiful view across the water, with the moss covered track sweeping away down the hill, and the little autumn flowers peeping from the ground in profuse flecks of colour. The trees, too, were beginning to turn and change shade. Above us little flecks of cloud drifted idly across the sky.

In the distance approaching us we saw a crowd of people. Snatches of sound were borne to us on the light wind. "We must conceal ourselves, Lobsang. It is the funeral of old Shang, the Silk Trader. A first class funeral. I should have attended, but I said I was too ill, and I shall lose face if they see me now." Huang had risen to his feet, and I rose as well from the boulder. Together we retreated a little way into the wood, where we could see, but not be seen. There was a rocky ridge, and we lay down behind it, Huang a little way behind me so that even if I were seen he would

175

not be. We made ourselves at ease, draping our robes around us, robes which blended well with the russet tints of autumn.

Slowly the funeral procession approached. The Chinese monks were gowned in yellow silk, with their rust red capes around their shoulders. The pale autumn sun shone on their freshly shaven heads, showing up the scars of the initiation ceremony; the sun gleamed on the silver bells they carried in their hands, making flashings and glintings as they were swung. The monks were singing the minor chant of the funeral service as they walked ahead of the huge Chinese lacquered coffin which was carried by thirty-two coolies. Attendants beat gongs, and let off fireworks to scare off any lurking devils, for, according to Chinese belief, demons were now ready to seize the soul of the deceased, and they had to be frightened off by fireworks and by noise. Mourners, with the white cloth of sorrow draped around their heads, walked behind. A woman, far advanced in pregnancy, and evidently a close relation, was weeping bitterly as she was helped along by others. Professional mourners wailed loudly as they shrieked the virtues of the departed to all who listened. Next came servants bearing paper money, and paper models of all the things which the deceased had in this life, and would need in the next. From where we watched, concealed by the ridge of rock, and by the overgrowing bushes, we could smell the incense and the scent of the freshly crushed flowers as they were trodden underfoot by the procession. It was a very big funeral indeed. Shang, the Silk Trader, must have been one of the leading citizens, for the wealth here was fabulous.

The party came slowly by us with loud wailings, and the clattering of cymbals, and the blaring of instruments, and the ringing of bells. Suddenly shadows came across the sun, and above the clamour of the funeral party we heard the drone of high-powered aero engines, a drone growing louder, and louder, and more and more ominous. Three sinister-looking Japanese planes came into view above the trees, between us and the sun. They circled around. One detached itself, and came lower, and swept right above the funeral procession. We were not perturbed. We thought that even the Japanese would respect the sanctity of death. Our hearts rose as the plane swept back to rejoin the other two, and together they made off. Our rejoicing was shortlived, however; the planes circled, and came at us again; little black dots fell from beneath their wings, and grew larger, and larger, as the shrieking bombs fell to earth, fell directly on the funeral procession.

Before us the trees swayed and rocked, the whole earth appeared to be in turmoil, riven metal went screaming by. So close were we that we heard no explosion. Smoke and dust, and shattered cyprus trees were in the air. Red lumps went swishing by, to land with sickening splats on anything in the way. For a moment all was hidden by a black and yellow pall of smoke. Then it was swept away by the wind, and we were left to face the ghastly carnage.

On the ground the coffin gaped wide, and empty. The poor dead body which it had contained was flung asprawl, like a broken doll, shredded, unkempt, discarded. We picked ourselves from the ground, shaken, and half stunned by the havoc, by the violence of the explosion, and by our very close escape. I stood and picked from the tree behind me a long sliver of metal which had barely missed me as it whirred by my head. The sharp end was dripping with blood, and it was hot, so hot that I dropped it with an exclamation of pain as I looked ruefully at my scorched finger tips.

On the rended trees pieces of cloth stirred in the breeze, cloth with bloody flesh adhering. An arm, complete with shoulder, still swayed across a forked branch some fifty feet away. It teetered, slipped, caught again for a moment on a lower branch, and then finally, sickeningly fell to earth. From somewhere a red, distorted head, grinning with frightened surprise, fell through the stripped branches of the trees, and rolled towards me, to finally stop at my feet as if it were gazing at me in awed wonder at the in-humanity of the Japanese aggressor.

It seemed a moment when even time itself stood still in horror. The air reeked with the odours of high explosive, with blood, and with riven guts. The only sounds were a swish and plop, as unmentionable things fell from the sky, or from the trees. We hurried to the wreckage, hoping that someone could be helped, sure that there must be some survivor of the tragedy. Here was a body, shredded and disembowelled, so mutilated, so scorched that we could not say if it was male or female; so mutilated that we could hardly say even that it was human. By it, across it, was a small boy, with his legs blown off at the thigh. He was whimpering with terror. As I knelt beside him he erupted a gout of bright blood, and coughed his life away. Sadly we looked about, and widened our area of search. Beneath a fallen tree we found the pregnant woman. The tree had been blown across her. It had burst her stomach. From her womb her unborn baby protruded, dead. Further along was a severed hand which still tightly grasped a silver bell. We searched and searched, and found no life.

From the sky came the sound of aircraft engines. The attackers were returning to view their ghastly work. We lay back on the blood-stained ground as the Japanese plane circled lower, and lower, to inspect the damage, to make sure that none lived to tell the tale. It turned lazily, banking like a hawk swooping for the kill, then came back, back in straight flight, lower and lower. The harsh crackle of machine-gun fire and the whiplash of bullets along the trees. Something tugged at the skirt of my robe and I heard a scream. I felt as if my leg had been scorched. "Poor Huang," I thought, "he's hit and he wants me." Above us the plane turned circling idly as if the pilot leaned as far as he could to view the ground below. He put his nose down,

178

and desultorily fired again and again, and circled once more. Apparently he was satisfied for he waggled his wings and went away. After a while I rose to give aid to Huang, but he was many feet away, quite unhurt, still half concealed in the ground. I pulled my robe and found my left leg had a scorch mark where the bullet had ploughed its way along the flesh. Inches from me the grinning skull now had a fresh bullet hole through it, straight through one temple and out through the other side; the exit hole was huge and had blown the brains out with it.

Once again we searched in the undergrowth and among the trees, but there was no sign of life. Fifty to a hundred people, perhaps more, had been here only minutes ago to pay homage to the dead. Now they too were dead. Now they were merely red ruin and shapeless mounds. We turned helplessly. There was nothing at all for us to do, nothing to save. Time alone would cover these scars.

This then was the "Fifteenth Day of the Eighth Month" when families came together at the ending of the day, when they came together with joy in their hearts at the reunion. Here at least, by the action of the Japanese, the families had "come together" at the ending of their day. We turned to continue our way, as we left the wrecked area a bird took up its interrupted song as if nothing at all had happened.

Life in Chungking at that time was crude indeed. Many money-grabbers had come in, people who tried to exploit the misery of the poor, who tried to capitalize on war. Prices were soaring, conditions were difficult. We were glad indeed when orders came through for us to resume our duties. Casualties near the coast had been very high indeed. Medical personnel were desperately needed. So once again, we left Chungking, and made our way down to the coast, where General Yo was waiting to give us our orders. Days later I was installed as medical officer in charge of the hospital, a laughable term indeed. The hospital was a collection of paddy fields in which the unfortunate patients lay on the water-logged ground, for there was nowhere else to lie, no bed, nothing. Our equipment? Paper bandages. Obsolete surgical apparatus, and anything else we could make, but at least we had the knowledge and the will to bring help to those so badly wounded, and of those we had a surfeit. The Japanese were winning everywhere. The casualties were ghastly.

One day the air-raids seemed to be more intense than usual. Bombs were dropping everywhere. The whole fields were ringed with bomb craters. Troops were retreating. Then in the evening of that day a contingent of Japanese rushed upon us, menacing us with their bayonets, jabbing first one, then another, just to show that they were the masters. We had no resistance, we had no weapons at all nothing with which to defend ourselves. The Japanese roughly questioned me as the one in charge, and then they went out in the fields to examine the patients. All the patients were ordered to stand up. Those who were too ill to walk and carry a load were bayoneted by the enemy then and there. The rest of us were marched off, just as we were, to a prison camp much further in the interior. We marched miles and miles each day. Patients were dropping dead by the roadside, and as they fell Japanese guards rushed to examine them for anything of value. Jaws clenched in death were prised open with a bayonet, and any gold fillings of teeth were crudely knocked out.

One day as we were marching along I saw that the guards in front had something strange on the end of their bayonets. They were waving them about. I thought it was some sort of celebration. It looked as if they had got balloons tied on the end of their rifles. Then, with laughs and shouts, guards came rushing down the line of prisoners, and we saw with a sick feeling in the stomach, that they had heads spiked to the end of their bayonets. Heads with the eyes open, the mouth open, too, the jaws dropped down. The Japanese had been taking prisoners, decapitating them, and spearing the necks as a sign—again—that they were the masters.

In our hospital we had been dealing with patients of all nations. Now, as we marched along, bodies of all nationalities were by the roadside. They were all of one nationality now, the nation of the dead. The Japanese had taken everything from them. For days we marched on, getting fewer, and fewer, getting tireder, and tireder, until those few of us who reached the new camp were stumbling along in a red haze of pain and fatigue, with the blood seeping through our rag-wrapped feet, and leaving a long red trail behind us. At last we reached the camp, and a very crude camp it was too. Here again the questioning started. Who was I? What was I? Why was I, a lama of Tibet, fighting on behalf of the Chinese? My reply to the effect that I was not fighting, but mending broken bodies, and helping those who were ill, brought abuse and blows. "Yes," they said, "yes, mending bodies so that they can fight against us."

At last I was put to work looking after those who were ill, trying to save them for the slave labour of the Japanese. About four months after we reached that camp there was a big inspection. Some high officials were coming to see how the prison camps were behaving, and whether there was anyone of note who could be of use to the Japanese. We were all lined up in the early dawn, and left standing there for hours, and hours, until the late afternoon, and a sorry crowd we looked by then. Those who fell from fatigue were bayoneted and dragged away to the death pile. We straightened our lines somewhat as high-powered cars drove up with a roar, and bemedalled men jumped out. A visiting Japanese major casually walked down the lines, looking over the prisoners. He glanced at me, then looked at me more carefully. He stared at me, and said something to me which I did not understand. Then as I did not reply he struck me across the face with the scabbard of his sword, cutting the skin. Quickly an orderly ran up to him. The major said something to him. The orderly ran off to the records office, and after a very short time he came back with my record. The major snatched it from him, and read it avidly. Then he shouted abuse at me, and issued an order to the guards with him. Once again I was knocked down by their rifle butts. Once again my nose—so newly repaired and rebuilt—was smashed and I was dragged away to their guard room. Here my hands and feet were tied behind my back, and pulled up and tied to my neck, so that every time I tried to rest my arms I nearly strangled myself. For a long time I was kicked and pummelled, and burned with cigarette ends while questions were shot at me. Then I was made to kneel, and guards jumped on my heels in the hope that that pain would compel me to answer. My arches snapped under the strain.

The questions they asked! How had I escaped? Whom had I spoken to while I was away? Did I know that it was an insult to their Emperor to escape? They also demanded details of troop movements because they thought that I, as a lama from Tibet, must know a lot about Chinese dispositions. Of course I did not answer, and they kept on burning me with their lighted cigarettes, and going through all the usual routine of torture. Eventually they put me on a crude sort of rack, and pulled the drum tight so that it felt as if my arms and legs were being dragged from their sockets. I fainted and each time I was revived by having a bucket of cold water thrown over me, and by being pricked with bayonet points. At last the medical officer in charge of the camp intervened. He said that if I had any more suffering I would assuredly die, and they would then not be able to get answers to their questions. They did not want to kill me, because to kill me would be to allow me to escape from their questions. I was dragged out by the neck, and thrown into a deep underground cell shaped like a bottle, made of cement. Here I was kept for days, it might have been weeks. I lost all count of time, there was no sensation of time. The cell was pitch dark. Food was thrown in every two days, and water was lowered in a tin. Often it was spilled, and I had to grovel in the dark, and scrabble with my hands to try and find it, or to try and find anything moist from the ground. My mind would have cracked under the strain, under that darkness so profound, but my training saved me. I thought again of the past.

Darkness? I thought of the hermits in Tibet, in their secure hermitages perched in lofty mountain peaks in inaccessible places among the clouds. Hermits who were immured in their cells, and stayed there for years, freeing the mind of the body, freeing the soul from the mind, so that they could realize greater spiritual freedom. I thought not of the present, but of the past, and during my reverie I inevitably came back to that most wonderful experience, my visit to the Chang Tang Highlands.

We, my Guide, the Lama Mingyar Dondup, and a few companions, and I, had set out from the golden roofed Potala in Lhasa in search of rare herbs. For weeks we had journeyed upwards, ever upwards into the frozen North, into Chang Tang Highlands, or, as some call it, Shamballah. This day we were nearing our objective. That day was indeed bitter, the bitterest of many frozen days. Ice blew at us driven by a shrieking gale. The frozen pellets struck our flapping robes, and abraded the skin from any surface which was left exposed. Here, nearly twenty-five thousand feet above the sea, the sky was a vivid purple, a few patches of cloud racing across were startling white in comparison. It looked like the white horses of the Gods, taking their riders across Tibet.

We climbed on, and on, with the terrain becoming more difficult with every step. Our lungs rasped in our throats. We clawed a precarious foothold in the hard earth, forcing our fingers into the slightest crack in the frozen rock. At last we reached that mysterious fog belt again (see *Third Eye*) and made our way through it with the ground

183

beneath our feet becoming warmer, and warmer, and the air around us becoming more and more balmy and comforting. Gradually we emerged from the fog into the lush paradise of that lovely sanctuary. Before us again was that land of a bygone age.

That night we rested in the warmth and comfort of the Hidden Land. It was wonderful to sleep on a soft bed of moss, and to breathe the sweet scent of flowers. Here in this land there were fruits which we had not tasted before, fruits which we sampled, and tried again. It was glorious, too, to be able to bathe in warm water, and to loll at ease upon a golden strand.

On the following day we journeyed onward, going higher, and higher, but now we were not at all troubled. We marched on through clumps of rhododendron, and passed by walnut trees, and others the names of which we did not know. We did not press ourselves unduly that day. Nightfall came upon us once again, but this time we were not cold. We were at ease, comfortable. Soon we sat beneath the trees, and lit our fire, and prepared our evening meal. With that completed we wrapped our robes about us, and lay and talked. One by one we dropped off to sleep.

Again on the next day we continued our march, but we had only covered two or three miles when suddenly, unexpectedly, we came to an open clearing, a spot where the trees ended, and before us—we stopped almost paralysed with amazement, shaking with the knowledge that we had come upon something completely beyond our understanding. We looked. The clearing before us was a vast one. There was a plain before us, more than five miles across. At its distant side there was an immense sheet of ice extending upwards, like a sheet of glass reaching towards the heavens, as if indeed it were a window on heaven, or a window on the past. For at the other side of that sheet of ice we could see, as if through the purest of water, a city, intact, a strange city, the like of which we had never seen even in the books of pictures which we had at the Potala.

Projecting from the glacier were buildings. Most of them were in a good state of preservation, because the ice had been thawed out gently in the warm air of the hidden valley, thawed out so gently, so gradually that not a stone or part of a structure had been damaged. Some of them, indeed, were quite intact, preserved throughout countless centuries by the wonderful pure dry air of Tibet. Some of those buildings, in fact, could have been erected perhaps a week before, they looked so new.

My Guide, the Lama Mingyar Dondup, broke our awed silence, saying, "My brothers, half a million years ago this was the home of the Gods. Half a million years ago this was a pleasant seaside resort in which lived scientists of a different race and type. They came from another place altogether, and I will tell you of their history one day, but through their experiments they brought calamity upon the earth, and they fled the scene of their disaster leaving the ordinary people of the earth behind. They caused calamity, and through their experiments the sea rose up and froze, and here before us we see a city preserved in the eternal ice from that time, a city which was inundated as the land rose, and the water rose with it, inundated and frozen."

We listened in fascinated silence as my Guide continued with his talk, telling us of the past, telling us of the ancient records far beneath the Potala, records engraved upon sheets of gold, just as now in the Western world records are preserved for posterity in what they called "time capsules."

Moved by a common impulse we rose to our feet, and then walked to explore the buildings within our reach. The closer we got, the more dumbfounded we became. It was all so very very strange. For a moment we could not understand the sensation that we felt. We imagined that we had suddenly become dwarfs. Then the solution hit us. The buildings were immense, as if they were built for a race

185

twice as tall as we. Yes, that was it. Those people, those super-people, were twice as tall as ordinary people of earth. We entered some of the buildings, and looked about. One in particular seemed to be a laboratory of some kind, and there were many strange devices, and many of them still worked.

A gushing current of ice cold water jerked me back to reality with stunning suddenness, jerked me back to the misery and pain of my existence in the stone oubliette. The Japanese had decided that I had been in there long enough, and I had not been "softened up" enough. The easiest way to get me out, they thought, was to fill the oubliette with water, so that I would float to the surface as a cork floats to the surface of a filled bottle. As I reached the top, reached the narrow neck of the cell, rough hands grabbed me and dragged me out. I was marched off to another cell, this time to one above ground, and flung in.

The next day I was put to work, again treating the sick. Later that week there was another inspection by the higher Japanese officials. There was much rushing about. The inspection was being carried out without any previous warning, and the guards were in a panic. I found myself at the time quite near the main gate of the prison. No one was taking any notice of me, so I took the opportunity to keep walking, not too fast, as I did not want to attract attention, but not too slow, either, it was not healthy to linger there! I kept walking, and walking, as if I had a perfect right to be out. One guard called to me, and I turned toward him, and raised my hand, as if in salute. For some reason he just waved back, and turned about his ordinary work. I continued with my walk. When I was out of sight of the prison, hidden by the bushes, I ran as fast as my weakened frame would enable me.

A few miles further on, I recollected, was a house owned by Western people whom I knew. I had, in fact, been able to do them some service in the past. So, cautiously, by nightfall, I made my way to their home. They took me in with warm exclamations of sympathy. They bandaged my many hurts, and gave me a meal, and put me to bed, promising that they would do everything they could to get me through the Japanese lines. I fell asleep, soothed by the thought that once again I was in the hands of friends.

Rough shouts and blows soon brought me back to reality, soon jerked me back from sleep. Japanese guards were standing over me, dragging me out of the bed, prodding me again with their bayonets. My hosts, after all their protestations of sympathy, had waited until I was asleep, and had then notified the Japanese guards that they had an escaped prisoner. The Japanese guards had lost no time in coming to collect me. Before I was taken away I managed to ask the Western people why they had so treacherously betrayed me. Their illuminating answer was, "You are not one of us. We have to look after our own people. If we kept you we should antagonize the Japanese, and endanger our work."

Back in that prison camp I was treated very badly indeed. For hours I was strung up from the branches of a tree, suspended by my two thumbs tied together. Then there was a sort of mock trial in front of the commandant of the camp. He was told, 'This man is a persistent escaper. He is causing us too much work." So he passed sentence on me. I was knocked down, and laid out on the ground. Then blocks were put beneath my legs so that my legs were supported clear of the ground. Two Japanese guards stood on each leg, and bounced, so that the bone snapped. I fainted with the agony of it. When I recovered consciousness I was back in the cold, dank, cell, with the rats swarming around me.

It was death not to attend the pre-dawn roll-call, and I knew it. A fellow prisoner brought me some bamboos, and I tied splints to each leg to support the broken bones. I used two other bamboos as crutches, and I had a third which I used as a sort of tripod leg in order to balance. With that

I managed to attend the roll-call, and so saved myself from death by hanging, or bayoneting, or disembowelling, or any other of the usual forms in which the Japanese specialised.

As soon as my legs were healed and the bones knit together—although not very well, as I had set them myself—the commandant sent for me, and told me that I was going to be moved to a camp yet further into the interior, where I was to be medical officer of this camp for women. So, once again, I was on the move. This time there was a convoy of lorries going to the camp and I was the only prisoner being moved there. So I was just ordered aboard, and kept chained like a dog near the tail board of one lorry. Eventually, several days later, we arrived at this camp where I was taken off and led to the commandant.

Here we had no medical equipment of any kind, and no drugs. We made what we could from old tins sharpened on stones, from fire-hardened bamboo, and from threads unravelled from tattered clothing. Some of the women had no clothing at all, or were very ragged. Operations were performed on conscious patients, and torn bodies were stitched with boiled cotton. Often by night the Japanese would come along and order out all women to inspect them. Any which they found to their liking they took off to the officers' quarters to entertain the permanent officers and any visitors. In the morning the women would be returned, looking shamefaced, and ill, and I as the prisoner-doctor would have to try to patch up their maltreated bodies.

CHAPTER TEN

How to Breathe

THE Japanese guards were in a bad mood again. Officers and men strode about the place scowling, striking at any unfortunate who happened to meet their gaze. We were glum indeed as we contemplated another day of terror, another day of food shortage and useless tasks. Hours before there had been a swirl of dust as a large captured American car pulled up with a jerk that would have torn the hearts of its makers. There were shouts and yells, and the running men buttoned their shabby uniforms. Guards rushed by, grabbing any bit of equipment that they could lay their hands on to make some sort of a show to indicate that they were efficient and doing their work.

It was a surprise visit from one of the generals commanding the area. Quite definitely it was a surprise. No one had even contemplated another inspection because there had been one only two days before. It seemed that sometimes in the camp the Japanese would call an inspection just to look over the women and to have parties. They would line up the women and examine them, and pick out the ones that they wanted, and these would be marched off under armed guard, and a little later we would hear anguished shrieks and cries of terror or pain. This time, though, it was the real thing, a genuine inspection, an inspection by a high-ranking general straight from Japan, who had come to see what was really happening in the camps. We found out later that the Japanese had been having a few setbacks, and it occurred to someone that if there were too many atrocities there may be retributions for a few officials later.

189

At last the guards were in a more or less straight line ready for inspection. There was much shuffling and clouds of dust were rising from the feet of the frightened men. We watched from behind our wire, interested, because this time the guards were being inspected and not the prisoners. For a long time the men were being lined up, and then at last there was an impression of tenseness, an impression that something was going to happen. As we watched we saw movements at the Guard House, men presenting arms. Then the general came out, swaggering along, and strutted down the line of men with his long sumurai sword trailing behind him. His face was distorted with rage at having been kept waiting, and his aides were all looking nervous and ill at ease. Slowly he went down the lines of men, picking out one here or there with whom to find fault. Nothing seemed to be right that day. Things were looking blacker and blacker.

The little "Sons of Heaven" were indeed a sorry-looking crew. In the hurry they picked up any equipment available no matter how unsuitable. They had lost their heads completely. They just HAD to show that they were doing something instead of lounging about wasting time. The general moved on, and then came to a sudden halt with a screech of rage. One man had a prisoner's drain-clearing pole with a tin on the end instead of his rifle. Some time before one of the prisoners had been using that pole and that tin to clear out our camp drains. The general looked at the man, and looked at the pole, and raised his head higher to look at the can at the end of the pole. He became more and more furious. He became quite inarticulate for a moment with rage. Already he had raised himself to his toes and given hard right and left face slaps to a number of men who had incurred his displeasure. Now at the sight of this drain-clearing pole he was completely overcome. Eventually he regained the power of movement, he jumped with rage, then looked about him for something with which to strike the man. A thought occurred to him. He looked down, unhooked his sword and scabbard, and brought that ornamental weapon down on the unfortunate guard's head with stunning force. The poor wretch buckled at the knees, and just dropped flat on the ground. Blood poured out of his nostrils, and out of his ears. The general contemptuously kicked him and motioned to the guards. The unfortunate man was picked up by his feet, and trailed along the ground, his head bumping and bumping. At last he disappeared from our sight, and he was not seen again in our camp.

Nothing at all seemed to go right with that inspection. The general and his accompanying officers found fault everywhere. They were turning a peculiar purple with rage. They carried out one inspection, and then they carried out another. We had never seen anything like it. But there was one bright spot from our point of view. The general was so irate with the guards that he forgot to inspect the prisoners. At last the high-ranking officers disappeared again into the Guard Room from whence came shouts of rage, and a shot or two. Then they came out again, climbed into their cars, and disappeared from our sight. The guards were given the order to fall out, and they dispersed still shaking with fright.

So—the Japanese guards were in a very bad mood. They had just beaten up a Dutch woman because she was large, and towered over them, and so made them feel inferior. As they said, she was taller than they, and that was an insult to their Emperor! She was knocked down with the butt of a rifle and kicked and prodded, so that she was injured internally and bleeding. For another hour or two, until sunset, she would have to remain on the ground outside the Guard Room at the main entrance. She would have to remain kneeling on the ground, kneeling with the blood pouring out her. No one, no matter how ill, could be moved before the guards gave permission. If a prisoner died, well,

191

that was one less to feed. Certainly the guards did not mind in the least, and die she did. Just before sunset she toppled over. No one could go to her aid. At last a guard motioned to two prisoners to come and drag away the body. They brought her to me, but it was useless. She was dead. She had bled to death.

It was difficult indeed treating patients under camp conditions. We lacked all supplies. Now our bandages were finished. They had been washed and washed, and used until they had rotted away, until the last few threads had failed to hang together. We could not make any more from clothing because no one had any to spare. Some of the prisoners, indeed, had no clothing at all. The matter was becoming quite acute. We had so many sores, so many wounds, and no method of treating them. In Tibet I had studied herbs, and on one of our work expeditions beyond the confines of the camp I had found a local plant that seemed quite familiar to me. It was wide with thick leaves, and it was a very useful astringent, a thing that we desperately needed. The problem was to get a supply of these leaves into the camp. A group of us talked it over, long into the night. Eventually it was decided that working parties must collect them somehow, and hide them in some unspecified manner when they were returning to camp. We discussed how they could be hidden. At last some really wise person suggested that as there was a working party collecting large bamboos, leaves could be hidden in the stems.

Women, or "girls" as they called themselves no matter their age, collected large quantities of fleshy leaves. I was delighted to see them. It was like greeting old friends. We spread all the leaves on the ground behind the huts. The Japanese guards looked on not at all worried about what we were doing. They thought that we had gone off our heads, or something, but we had to spread the leaves so that they could be sorted carefully, because all kinds had been brought in by the women who were not used to picking

192

one particular plant, and only the one variety could be used. We picked over the leaves, and sorted out the one type that we wanted. The rest—well, we had to get rid of those as well, and we spread them upon the pile of dead at the edge of our compound.

The leaves left were sorted into large and small, and carefully cleaned from the dirt on them. We had no water in which to wash them, because water was a very scarce commodity. Now we had to find a suitable container in which to mash the leaves. The camp rice bowl was the largest thing available, so we took that and put the carefully picked leaves in it. The next worry was finding a suitable stone, one with sharp points on it so that the leaves could be macerated, and made into a fine pulp. Eventually we were able to find a stone such as we required. It was a stone requiring two hands to lift it. The women who were helping me took it in turns to stir and pound leaves until they were reduced to a sticky green dough.

Our next problem was to find something to absorb blood and pus while the astringent was acting, and something to hold the mass together. Bamboo is a plant of many uses; we decided to put that plant to yet another use. From old canes and waste wood material we scraped a pith, and dried it over a fire in tins. When quite dry it became as fine as flour, and more absorbent than cotton wool. Half bamboo pith and half mashed leaves made a highly satisfactory mixture. Unfortunately it was friable and fell to pieces at a touch.

The construction of a base on which to lay the compound was not easy. We had to shred the outer fibres off the young green bamboo shoots, and tease them apart carefully so that we obtained the longest possible threads. These we laid on a thoroughly scrubbed metal sheet, which normally protected the floor from the fire. We laid the fibres on lengthwise and crisscross, as if we were weaving, as if we were making a long, narrow carpet. Eventually, after much toil, we had an untidy-looking net about eight feet long by two feet wide.

With a rolling pin made of large diameter bamboo we forced the leaf and pith mixture into the network, pushing it in so that all the strands of the bamboo were covered, till we had a fairly even filling of our mashed mixture. Then we turned it over and did the same with the other side. When we finished we had a pale green dressing with which to staunch the flow of blood and promote healing. It had been something like paper-making, and the finished result was similar to thick green cardboard, pliable, not easily bent, indeed not easily cut with the crude implement which we had at our disposal. But eventually we did manage to cut the material into strips about four inches wide, and then we peeled them from the metal plate to which they had been adhering. In their present state they would keep and remain flexible for many weeks. We found them a blessing indeed.

One day a woman who had been working in the Japanese canteen pretended that she was ill. She came to me in a state of great excitement. She had been cleaning out a store-room containing much equipment captured from the Americans. Somehow she had knocked over a tin from which the label had fallen, and some red-brown crystals had poured out. Idly she had poked her fingers into them, stirring them round, wondering what they were. Later, on putting her hands into water to continue scrubbing, she had found ginger-brown stains on her hands. Was she poisoned? Was it a trap of the Japanese? She had decided that she had better come to me in a hurry. I looked at her hands, I sniffed them, and then if I had been emotional I should have jumped for joy. It was obvious to me what caused the stains. Permanganate of potash crystals, just the thing we needed for our many tropical ulcer cases. I said, "Nina, you get that tin out somehow. Fix the lid on and put the tin in a bucket, but get it here, and keep it dry." She returned to the canteen absolutely bubbling over with joy to think that she had been responsible for discovering something which would alleviate a little of the suffering. Later in the day she returned and produced a tin of crystals, and a few days after she produced another, and yet another tin. We blessed the Americans that day. We even blessed the Japanese for capturing the American supplies!

Tropical ulcers are dreadful things. Lack of adequate food and neglect are the main causes. It may be that the inability to have a good wash contributes toward it. First there is a slight itch, and the victim absent-mindedly scratches. Then a small pimple like a red pin-head appears, and it is scratched or dug with exasperation. Infection from the finger nails gets into the abrasion. Gradually the whole area becomes red, an angry red. Little yellow nodules form beneath the skin and cause further irritation, and more severe scratching. The ulcer would grow outwards, and downwards. Pus, evil smelling stuff, would appear. In course of time the body resources would become further depleted, and the health would deteriorate even more. Down, and down, would grow the ulcer, eating through the flesh, through the cartilage, and eventually through the bone, killing the marrow and the tissue. If nothing was done the patient would eventually die.

But something had to be done. The ulcer, the source of the infection, had to be removed somehow and as quickly as possible. Lacking all medical equipment we had to resort to truly desperate measures. The ulcer had to be removed to save the life of the patient, the whole thing had to be lifted out. So—there was only one thing for it. We made a scoop from a tin, and carefully sharpened the edge. Then we sterilised the tin the best way we could over the flame of our fire. Fellow prisoners held the affected limb of the sufferer, and with the sharpened tin I would scoop out the dead flesh and the pus, until only clean healthy tissue was left. We had to be quite sure that no spot of infection was overlooked and left behind, or the ulcer would grow again like a malignant weed. With the tissue cleansed of the ulcer's ravages the large cavity would be filled with the herbal paste, and with infinite care the patient would be nursed back to health—health as measured by our camp standard! And that standard would be almost death anywhere else. This permanganate of potash would help the healing process by assisting in keeping down pus and other sources of infection. We treated it like gold dust.

So our treatment sounds brutal? It was! But our "brutal" methods saved many a life, and many a limb too. Without such treatment the ulcer would grow, and grow, poisoning the system, so that eventually the arm or leg had to be amputated (without anaesthetics!) to save the life of the sufferer. Health was indeed a problem in our camp. The Japanese gave us no assistance of any kind, so in the end I drew upon my knowledge of breathing, and taught many of those in the camp special breathing for special purposes because by breathing correctly, breathing to certain rhythms, one can do much to improve the health both mentally and physically.

My Guide, the Lama Mingyar Dondup, taught me the science of breathing after he had caught me one day panting up a hill almost collapsing with exhaustion. "Lobsang, Lobsang," he said, "what have you been doing to get yourself in that horrible state?" "Honourable Master," I replied gaspingly, "I have been trying to walk up the hill on stilts." He looked at me sadly, and shook his head with an air of sad resignation. He sighed and motioned for me to sit down. For a time there was silence between us— silence, that is, except for the rasping of my breath as I strove to get back to normalcy.

I had been walking about down near the Linghor Road on stilts, showing off to the pilgrims—showing off by boasting how the monks of Chakpori could walk better, and further, and faster on stilts than anyone else in Lhasa. To prove the matter even more conclusively I had turned, and

196

run on stilts up the hill. As soon as I had managed to turn the first bend and was out of sight of the pilgrims I had fallen off with sheer exhaustion, and just after my Guide had come along and seen me in that sorry plight.

"Lobsang, it is indeed time that you learned some more. There has been enough play, enough sport. Now, as you have so clearly demonstrated, you are in need of instruction on the science of correct breathing. Come with me. We will see what we can do to remedy that state of affairs." He rose to his feet, and led the way up the hill. I rose reluctantly, picked up my stilts which had fallen askew, and followed him. He strode on easily, seeming to glide. There was no effort in his movement at all, and I, many years younger, struggled on after him, panting away like a dog on a hot summer's day.

At the top of the hill we turned into the enclosure of our lamasery, and I followed my Guide to his room. Inside we seated ourselves on the floor in the usual way, and the lama rang for the inevitable tea without which no Tibetan can carry on a serious discussion! We kept silence while the serving monks came in with tea and tsampa, and then as they left the lama poured out the tea, and gave me my first instruction on the art of breathing, instruction which was to be invaluable to me in this prison camp.

"You are puffing and panting away like an old man, Lobsang," he said. "I will soon teach you to overcome that, because no one should work so hard at what is an ordinary, natural, everyday occurrence. Too many people neglect breathing. They think you just take in a load of air, and expel that load of air, and take in another." "But, Honourable Master," I replied, "I have been able to breathe quite nicely for nine years or more. How else can I breathe but the way in which I have always managed?" "Lobsang, you must remember that breath is indeed the source of life. You can walk, and you can run, but without breath you can do neither. You must learn a new system, and first of all

197

you must take a standard of time in which to breathe, because until you know this standard of time there is no way in which you can apportion the various ratios of time to your breathing, and we breathe at different rates for different purposes." "He took my left wrist and pointed out a spot saying "Take your heart, your pulse. Your pulse goes in the rhythm of one, two, three, four, five, six. Put your finger on your pulse yourself, and feel, and then you will understand what I am talking about." I did so; I put a finger on my left wrist and felt my pulse rate as he said, one, two, three, four, five, six. I looked up at my Guide as he continued, "If you think about it you will find that you breathe in air for as long as your heart takes to beat six times. But that is not good enough. You will have to be able to vary that breathing quite a lot, and we will deal with that in a few moments." He paused and looked at me, and then said, "Do you know, Lobsang, you boys—I have been watching you at play—get yourselves really exhausted because you do not know the first thing about breathing. You think that as long as you take in air and let out air that is all that matters. You could not be more incorrect. There are four main methods of breathing, so let us examine them and see what they have to offer us, see what they are. The first method is a very poor one indeed. It is known as top breathing, because in this system only the upper part of the chest and lungs is used, and that as you should know is the smallest part of your breath cavity, so when you do this top breathing you get very little air into your lungs, but you get a lot of stale air in the deepest recesses. You see, you make only the top of your chest move. The bottom part of your chest and your abdomen are stationary, and that is a very bad thing indeed. Forget about top breathing, Lobsang, because it is quite useless. It is the worst form of breathing one can do, and we must turn to others."

He paused, and turned to face me, saying, "Look, this is top breathing. Look at the strained position I have to adopt. But that, as you will find later, is the type of breathing done by most Westerners, by most people outside Tibet and India. It causes them to think in a woolly manner, and to be mentally lethargic." I looked at him in open-mouthed amazement. I certainly did not imagine that breathing was such a difficult affair. I thought that I had always managed reasonably well, and now I was learning that I was wrong. "Lobsang, you are not paying much attention to me. Now let us deal with the second system of breathing. This is known as middle breathing. It is not a very good form either. There is no point in dealing with it more fully because I do not want you to use it, but when you get to the West, you will hear people refer to it as rib breathing, or breathing in which the diaphragm is kept stationary. The third system of breathing is low breathing, and while it is possibly a little better than the other two systems it still is not correct. Some people call this low breathing abdominal breathing. In this system the lungs do not get completely filled with air. The air in the lungs is not completely replaced, and so again there is staleness, bad breath, and illness. So do nothing at all about these systems of breathing, but do as I do, do as other lamas here do, the Complete Breath, and here is how you should do it." "Ah!" I thought, "now we are getting down to it, now I am going to learn something, now why did he tell me all that other stuff, and then say I mustn't do it?" "Because, Lobsang," my Guide said—obviously having read my thoughts—"because you should know faults as well as virtues. Since you have been here at Chakpori," said my Guide, the Lama Mingyar Dondup, "you have undoubtedly noticed that we stress and stress again the importance of keeping one's mouth shut. That is not merely so that we can make no false statements, but so that one can breathe only through the nostrils. If you breath through the mouth you lose the advantage of air filters in the nostrils, and of the temperature control mechanism which the human body has. And again, if you

199

persist in breathing through the mouth the nostrils eventually become stopped up, and so one gets catarrh and a stuffy head, and a whole host of other complaints." I guiltily became aware that I was watching my Guide with open-mouthed amazement. Now I closed my mouth with such a snap that his eyes twinkled with amusement, but he said nothing about that; instead he continued, "Nostrils really are very important things, and they must be kept clean. If ever your nostrils become unclean, sniff a little water up them, and let it run down inside the mouth so that you can expel it through the mouth. But whatever you do, do not breathe through the mouth, but only through the nostrils. It might help, by the way, if you use warm water. Cold water may make you sneeze." He turned, and touched the bell at his side. A servant entered and refilled the tea jug and brought fresh tsampa. He bowed, and left us. After a few moments the Lama Mingyar Dondup resumed his discourse to me. "Now, Lobsang, we will deal with the true method of breathing, the method which has enabled certain of the lamas of Tibet to prolong their life to a truly remarkable span. Let us deal with Complete Breathing. As the name implies it embodies the other three systems, low breathing, middle breathing, and top breathing, so the lungs are truly filled with air, and the blood is therefore purified, and filled with life force. This is a very easy system of breathing. You have to sit, or stand, in a reasonably comfortable position and breathe through the nostrils. I saw you just a few moments ago, Lobsang, crouched over, absolutely slouching, and you just cannot breathe properly when you are slouched over. You must keep your spine upright. That is the whole secret of correct breathing." He looked at me, and sighed, but the twinkle in the corners of his eyes belied the depth of the sigh! Then he got up, and walked across to me, put his hands beneath my elbows, and lifted me up so that I was sitting quite upright. "Now, Lobsang, that's how you must sit, like that, with your spine upright, with your abdomen under control, with your arms at your sides. Now sit like that. Expand your chest, force your ribs outwards, and then push down your diaphragm so that the lower abdomen protrudes also. In that way you will have a complete breath. There is nothing magical about it, you know, Lobsang. It is just ordinary common-sense breathing. You have to get as much air in you as you can, and then you have to get all the air out again and replace it. For the moment you may feel that this is involved or intricate, you may feel that it is too difficult, not worth the effort, but it IS worth the effort. You feel that it is not because you are lethargic, because you have got into a somewhat slovenly way of breathing of late, and you have to have breath discipline." I breathed as directed, and to my considerable astonishment I found that it was easier. I found that my head swam a little for the first few seconds, and then it was easier still. I could see colours more clearly, and even in the few minutes I felt better.

"I am going to give you some breathing exercises every day, Lobsang, and I am going to ask you to keep on at it. It is worthwhile. You will have no more trouble with getting out of breath. That little jaunt up the hill distressed you, but I who am many times your age can come up without difficulty." He sat back, and watched me while I breathed in the way he had instructed. Certainly I could even now at this early stage appreciate the wisdom of what he was saying. He settled himself again and continued: "The only purpose of breathing no matter what system one adopts, is to take in as much air as possible, and to distribute it throughout the body in a different form, in a form which we call prana. That is the life force itself. That prana is the force which activates man, which activates everything that lives, plants, animals, man, even the fishes have to extract oxygen from water and convert it to prana. However, we are dealing with your breathing, Lobsang. Inhale slowly. Retain that breath for a few seconds. Then exhale quite

201

slowly. You will find that there are various ratios of inhaling, holding, exhaling, which accomplish various effects such as cleansing, vitalising, etc. Perhaps the most important general form of breathing is what we call the cleansing breath. We will go into this now, because from now on I want you to do it at the beginning and ending of every day, and at the beginning and ending of every particular exercise." I had been following very carefully. I knew well the power that these high lamas had, how they could glide across the earth faster than a man could gallop on a horse, and how they could arrive at their destination untroubled, serene, controlled, and I determined that long before I too was a lama—for at this stage I was just an acolyte—I would master the science of breathing.

My Guide, the Lama Mingyar Dondup, continued, "Now, Lobsang, for this cleansing breath. Inhale completely, three complete breaths. No, not shallow little things like that. Deep breaths, really deep ones, the deepest that you can manage, fill your lungs, draw yourself up and let yourself become full of air. That is right," he said. "Now with the third breath retain that air for some four seconds, screw up your lips as if you were going to whistle, but do not puff out the cheeks. Blow a little air through the opening in your lips with all the vigour that you can. Blow it out hard, let it go free. Then stop for a second, retaining the air which is left. Blow out a little more, still with all the vigour you can muster. Stop for another second, and then blow out the remainder so that there is not a puff of air left inside your lungs. Blow it out as hard as you can. Remember you MUST exhale in this case with very considerable vigour through the opening in your lips. Now, do you not find that this is remarkably refreshing?" To my surprise I had to agree. It had seemed to me a bit stupid just puffing out and blowing out, but now that I had tried it a few times I really found that I was tingling with energy, feeling perhaps better than I had ever felt before. So I huffed, and I puffed, and I expanded myself, and I blew my cheeks out. Then suddenly I felt my head swimming. It seemed to me that I was getting lighter, and lighter. Through the haze I heard my Guide, "Lobsang, Lobsang, stop! You must not breathe like that. Breathe as I tell you. Do not experiment, for to do so is dangerous. Now you have got yourself intoxicated through breathing incorrectly, by breathing too quickly. Exercise only as I am telling you to exercise, for I have the experience. Later you can experiment on your own. But, Lobsang, always caution those whom you are teaching to be careful to follow the exercises, and not to experiment. Tell them never to experiment with different ratios of breathing unless they have a competent teacher with them, for to experiment with breathing is dangerous indeed. To follow the set exercise is safe, it is healthy, and no harm at all can fall to those who breathe as instructed."

The lama stood up, and said, "Now, Lobsang, it will be a good idea if we increase your nervous force. Stand erect as I am standing now. Inhale as much as you can, then when you think that your lungs are full force in yet a little more breath. Slowly exhale. Slowly. Refill your lungs completely, and retain that breath. Extend your arms straight in front of you, not using any effort, you know, just to keep your arms in front of you with just enough strength to keep them horizontal, but use as little effort as you can. Now, look, watch me. Draw your hands back toward the shoulder, gradually contracting the muscles and making them tight so that by the time your hands can touch your shoulders the muscles will be quite taut, and the fists clenched. Watch me, see how I am clenching mine. Clench your hands so tightly that they tremble with the effort. Still keeping the muscles taut push the fists slowly out, then draw them back rapidly several times, perhaps half a dozen times. Exhale vigorously, really vigorously as I told you before, with the mouth, with the lips pursed up, and with just a hole through which you blow the breath as strongly as you can. After you have done that a few times finish by practising the cleansing breath once again." I tried it, and I found it as before of great benefit to me. Besides it was fun, and I was always ready for fun! My Guide broke in on my thoughts. "Lobsang, I want to emphasize, and emphasize again, that the speed of the drawing back of the fists and then tension of the muscles determines how much benefit you can get from this. Naturally you will have made quite sure that your lungs are absolutely full before doing this exercise. This, by the way, is a truly invaluable exercise, and will help you enormously during later years."

He sat down and watched me go through that system, gently correcting my faults, praising me when I did it well, and when he was satisfied he made me go through all the exercises again to be quite sure that I could do it without further instruction. Eventually he motioned for me to sit beside him while he told me how the Tibetan system of breathing was formed after deciphering the old records deep down in the caverns beneath the Potala.

Later in my studies I was taught various things about breath, for we of Tibet do not cure only by herbs, but we also cure through the patient's breathing. Breathing is indeed the source of life, and it may be of interest to give a few notes here which may enable those who have some ailment, perhaps of long standing, to banish or to alleviate their suffering. It can be done through correct breathing, you know, but do remember—breathe only as advised in these pages, for to experiment is dangerous unless there is a competent teacher at hand. To experiment blindly is folly indeed.

Disorders of the stomach, the liver, and the blood, can be overcome by what we term the "retained breath." There is nothing magical in this, mind, except in the result, and the result can appear to be quite magical, quite without parallel. But—at first you must stand erect, or if you are in bed, lie straight. Let us assume, though, that you are out of bed and can stand erect. Stand with your heels together, with your shoulders back and your chest out. Your lower abdomen will be tightly controlled. Inhale completely, take in as much air as you can, and keep it in until you feel a slight—very slight—throbbing in your temples to the left and to the right. As soon as you feel that exhale vigorously through the open mouth, REALLY vigorously, you know, not just letting it drift out, but blowing it out through the mouth with all the force at your command. Then you must do the cleansing breath. There is no point in going into that again because I have told you about that as my Guide, the Lama Mingyar Dondup, told me. I will just reiterate that the cleansing breath is absolutely invaluable to enable you to improve your health.

Before we can do anything about breathing we must have a rhythm, a unit of time which represents a normal inhalation. I have already mentioned it as it was taught to me, but perhaps repetition in this case will be a useful thing as it will help to fix it permanently in one's mind. The heart beat of the person is the proper rhythmic standard for that particular individual's breathing. Hardly anyone has the same standard of course, but that does not matter. You can find your normal breathing rhythm by placing your finger on your pulse and counting. Put your right-hand fingers on your left wrist and feel about for the pulse. Let us assume that it is an average of one, two, three, four, five, six. Get that rhythm firmly fixed in your sub-conscious so that you know it unconsciously, sub-consciously, so that you do not have to think about it. It does not matter—to repeat—what your rhythm is as long as you know it, as long as your sub-conscious knows it, but we are imagining that your rhythm is the average one in which the air intake lasts for six beats of your heart. This is just the ordinary work-a-day routine. We are going to alter that breathing rate quite a lot for various purposes. There is nothing difficult in it.

It is a very easy thing indeed which can lead to spectacular results in improved health. All acolytes of the higher grade in Tibet were taught breathing. We had certain exercises which we had to do before studying anything else, and this was the preliminary procedure in all cases. Would YOU like to try it! Then first of all sit erect, you can stand if you like, but there is no point in standing if you can sit. Inhale slowly the complete breathing system. That is, chest and abdomen while counting six pulse units. That is quite easy, you know. You only have to keep a finger on the pulse in your wrist and let your heart pump out once, twice, three, four, five, six times. When you have got the breath in after your six pulse units, retain it while your heart beats three times. After that exhale through the nostrils for six heart beats. That is, for the same time as that in which you inhaled. Now that you have exhaled keep your lungs empty for three pulse units, and then start all over again. Repeat this as many times as you like but—do not tire yourself. As soon as you feel any tiredness, stop. You should never tire yourself with exercises because if you do you defeat the whole object of those exercises. They are to tone one up and make one feel fit, not to run one down or to make one tired.

We always started with the cleansing breath exercise, and that cannot be done too often. It is completely harmless and is most beneficial. It rids the lungs of stale air, rids them of impurities, and in Tibet there is no T.B.! So you can do the cleansing breath exercises whenever you feel like it, and you will get the greatest benefit from it.

One extremely good method of acquiring mental control is by sitting erect, and inhaling one complete breath. Then inhale one cleansing breath. After that inhale in the ratio of one, four, two. That is (let us have seconds for a change!) inhale for five seconds, then hold your breath for four times five seconds, that is, twenty seconds. When you have done that breathe out for ten seconds. You can cure

206

yourself of a lot of pain by breathing properly, and this is a very good method; if you have some pain either lie down, or sit erect, it does not matter which. Then breathe rhythmically, keeping the thought in your mind that with each breath the pain is disappearing, with each exhalation the pain is being pushed out. Imagine that every time you breathe in you are breathing in the life force which is displacing the pain. Imagine that every time you breathe out you are pushing out the pain. Put your hand over the affected part, and imagine that with your hand with every breath you are wiping the cause of pain away. Do this for seven complete breaths. Then try the cleansing breath, and after that rest for a few seconds, breathing slowly and normally. You will probably find that the pain has either completely gone, or has so much lessened that it does not bother you. But if for any reason you still have the pain, repeat the same thing, try the same thing once, or twice more until eventually relief comes. You will of course quite understand that if it is an unexpected pain, and if it recurs, you will have to ask your doctor about it because pain is nature's warning that something is wrong, and while it is perfectly correct and permissible to lessen pain when one is aware of it, it is still essential that one does something to find out what caused the pain, and to cure the cause. Pain should never be left untended.

If you are feeling tired, or if there has been a sudden demand on your energies, here is the quickest way to recuperate. Once again it doesn't matter if you are standing or sitting, but keep your feet close together, toes and heels touching. Then clasp your hands together so that your fingers of each hand interlock, and so that your hands and feet each form a sort of closed circle. Breathe rhythmically for a few times, rather deep breaths, and slow in the exhaling. Then pause for three pulse units, and next do the cleansing breath. You will find that your tiredness has gone.

Many people are very, very nervous indeed when going

for an interview. They get clammy palms and perhaps shaky knees. There is no need for anyone to be like that because it is so easy to overcome, and this is a method of doing it while you are, perhaps, in the waiting room, possibly at the dentist! Take a really deep breath, breathing through your nostrils of course, and hold that breath for ten seconds. Then exhale slowly with the breath under full control all the time. Allow yourself to take two or three ordinary breaths, and then again inhale deeply taking ten seconds to fill your lungs. Hold the breath again, and exhale slowly, again taking ten seconds. Do this three times, as you can without anyone noticing, and you will find that you are absolutely reassured. The pounding of your heart will have stopped and you will feel much strengthened in confidence. When you leave that waiting room and go to your place of interview you will find that you are in control of yourself. If you feel a flutter or two of nervousness, then— take a deep breath and hold it for a second or so, as you can easily do while the other man is talking. This will reinforce your flagging confidence. All Tibetans use systems such as this. We also used breath control when lifting, because the easiest way to lift anything, it may be furniture, or lifting a heavy bundle, the easiest way is to take a really deep breath and hold it while you lift. When the actual act of lifting is over, then you can let out your breath slowly and continue to breathe in the normal way. Lifting while you hold a deep breath is easy. It is worth trying for yourself. It is worth trying to lift something fairly heavy with your lungs full of air and see the difference.

Anger, too, is controlled by that deep breathing, and by holding the breath and exhaling slowly. If for any reason you feel really angry—justly or otherwise!—take a deep breath. Hold it for a few seconds, and then expel that breath quite slowly. You will find that your emotion is under control, and you are master (or mistress) of the situation. It is very harmful to give way to anger and to

208

irritation, because that can lead to gastric ulcers. So— remember this breathing exercise of taking a deep breath, retaining it, and then expelling slowly.

You can do all these exercises with absolute confidence, knowing that they just cannot harm you in any way, but— a word of warning—keep to these exercises, and do not try anything more advanced except under the guidance of a competent teacher, because ill advised breathing exercises can do quite a lot of harm. In our prison camp we had our prisoners breathe like this. We also went far more deeply into the matter, and taught them to breathe so that they would not feel pain, and that, allied with hypnosis, enabled us to do deep abdominal operations and to amputate arms and legs. We had no anaesthetics, and so we had to resort to this method of killing pain—hypnosis and breath control. That is nature's method, the natural way.

CHAPTER ELEVEN

The Bomb

THE days crawled by with soul-searing monotony, lengthening into weeks, spreading into months, into years. At last there came a diversion from the everyday sameness of treating those who were afflicted. One day the guards came hurrying around with sheaves of paper in their hands, beckoning to a prisoner here, to a prisoner there. I was on that list. We were assembled on the square facing our huts. We were kept for some hours just standing idly, and then, as the day had almost ended, the commandant came before us and said, "You trouble-makers, you who have insulted our Emperor, you are going elsewhere for further treatment. You will leave in ten minutes." He turned abruptly and marched away. We stood more or less stunned. Ready in ten minutes? Well, at least we had no possessions. All we had to do was to say a few hurried farewells and then return to the compound.

So we were going to be taken to another camp? We speculated on the sort of camp, on where it would be. But, as is inevitable in such cases, no one had any really constructive thought. At the end of ten minutes whistles were blown, guards came hurrying around again, and we were marched off, some three hundred of us. We marched out through the gates; we left full of wonder, full of speculation, what sort of camp would this be? We were acknowledged trouble-makers. We had never given in to the Japanese blandishments. We knew them for what they were. We knew, though, that wherever we were going it was not to a pleasant camp.

We marched past soldiers going the other way. They appeared to be in a high state of humour. No wonder, we thought, because according to the reports reaching us the Japanese were winning everywhere. Soon, we were told, they would be in control of the whole world. How mistaken they were! At that time though we could only believe what the Japanese told us, we had no other source of information. These soldiers were most aggressive as they passed by and they lost no opportunity of dealing a blow at us—striking out wildly, irrationally, just for the sheer joy of hearing a rifle butt thud on shrinking flesh. We marched on, driven on by the curses of the guards. They too freely used their rifle butts. All too frequently the sick fell by the wayside where they were belaboured by the guards. If they could not regain their feet and stumble on blindly perhaps supported by others, then the guards stepped up and a bayonet thrust would end the struggle. Sometimes though the guard would decapitate the poor victim and stick the severed head on the end of his bayonet. He would then run up and down the lines of toiling prisoners, grinning fiendishly at our looks of horror.

Eventually, after many days of tiring, gruelling marching, with far too little food, we arrived at a small port and were driven into a rude camp which had been constructed by the harbour. Here there were a number of men, men of all nations, trouble-makers like us. They were so apathetic with weariness and with ill-treatment that they hardly looked up as we entered. Our number was now sadly reduced. Of three hundred or so who had started out only about seventy-five arrived. That night we stayed sprawled on the ground in the encampment behind barbed wire. There was no shelter for us, no privacy, but we were used to that by now. Men and women lay on the ground, or did what they had to do under the eyes of the Japanese guards who kept searchlights trained upon us for every moment of that long night.

In the morning we had a roll-call, and then we were kept standing in a ragged line for two or three hours. Eventually the guards condescended to come and march us out, march us further down to the harbour, to a quay where there was a rusty old tramp ship, a really derelict affair. I was not by any means an expert on shipping. In fact almost every one of the prisoners knew more about nautical affairs than I, yet even to me this ship looked as if at any moment it would sink at its moorings. We were marched aboard along a creaking, rotted gang plank which also threatened to collapse at any moment and throw us into the scummy sea, which was littered with debris, floating boxes, empty tins, bottles, dead bodies.

As we boarded the ship we were forced down a hold in the forward part. Some three hundred of us were there. There was not enough room for us to sit down, certainly not enough room to move around. The last of the party was forced down with blows of rifle butts, and with the curses of the Japanese guards. Then came a clang as if the Gates of Doom were closing upon us. The cover of the hatch was slammed down, sending clouds of stinking dust

211

upon us. We heard the sound of mallets driving home wooden wedges, and all light was excluded. After what seemed to be a terribly long time the ship started to vibrate. There was the creaking rumble of the derelict old engine. It really felt as if the whole framework would shake itself to pieces and drop us out through the bottom of the ship. From the deck we could hear muffled shouts and screamed instructions in Japanese. The chugging continued. Soon there was a terriffic rolling and pitching which told us that we had gone beyond the harbour and had reached the open sea. The journey was very rough indeed. The sea must have been tumultuous. We were continually thrown against each other, toppled over to be trampled on by others. We were shut down in the hold of that cargo boat and allowed on deck once only, during the hours of darkness. For the first two days no food at all was given to us. We knew why. It was to make sure that our spirit was broken. But it had little effect upon us. After two days we had about a cupful of rice each for each day.

Many of the weaker prisoners soon died in the suffocating stench, shut down in that stinking hold. There was not enough oxygen to keep us alive. Many died, and collapsed like broken discarded dolls upon the steel floor beneath us. We, the hardly more fortunate survivors, had no choice but to stand on the dead and decomposing bodies. The guards would not allow us to move them out. We were all prisoners, and it did not matter to the guards whether we were dead or alive, we had to be the correct number as shown on their papers. So the rotting dead had to be kept in the hold with the suffering living until we arrived at our port of destination, when bodies dead and alive would be counted.

We lost all track of days, but eventually after an unspecified time there was a change in the note of the engine. The pitching and tossing lessened. The vibration altered and we surmised correctly that we were approaching a harbour.

212

After much noise and fuss there came the clatter of chains, and the anchors were dropped. After what seemed to be an interminable time the hatches were flung off and Japanese guards started to descend with a Japanese port medical officer with them. Half way down they stopped in disgust. The Medical Officer vomited with the stench, vomited over us beneath. Then throwing dignity to the winds, they beat a hasty retreat up to the deck.

The next thing we knew was that hoses were being brought and streams of water rained down upon us. We were half drowned. The water was rising to our waists, our chests, to our chins, floating particles of the dead, the rotted dead, to our mouths. Then there were shouts and exclamations in Japanese and the water flow stopped. One of the deck officers came and peered over, and there was much gesticulation and discussion. He said that the boat would sink if any more water was pumped in. So a larger hose was dropped in and all the water was pumped out again.

All that day and all that night we were kept down there, shivering in our wet rags, sick with the stench of the decayed dead. The next day we were allowed up, two or three at a time. Eventually my turn came, and I went up on deck. I was roughly questioned. Where was my identity disc? My name was checked against a list, and I was roughly shoved over the side into a barge which was already crowded, and overcrowded, with a shivering collection of humanity, living scarecrows clad in the last vestiges of clothing. Some, indeed, were not clad at all. At last with the gunwales awash and with the barge threatening to sink if another person was put aboard, the Japanese guards decided that no more could safely be crammed in. A motor boat chugged up to the bows and a rope was made fast. The motor boat started for the shore dragging us in the decrepit old barge behind.

That was my first sight of Japan. We had reached the

213

Japanese mainland and once ashore we were put into an open camp, a camp upon waste ground surrounded by barbed wire. For a few days we were kept there while the guards interrogated each man and woman, and then eventually a number of us were segregated and marched off a few miles into the interior where there was a prison which had been kept vacant to await our arrival.

One of the prisoners, a white man, gave way under the torture and said that I had been helping prisoners escape, that I had military information given me by dying prisoners. So once again I was called in for interrogations. The Japanese were most enthusiastic about trying to make me talk. They saw from my record that all previous attempts had failed, so this time they really excelled themselves. My nails, which had regrown, were split off backwards and salt was rubbed into the raw places. As that still did not make me speak I was suspended by my two thumbs from a beam and left for a whole day. That made me very sick indeed, but the Japanese were still not satisfied. The rope suspending me was cast loose, and I dropped with a bone shaking thud to the hard floor of the compound. A rifle butt was jammed in my chest. Guards knelt upon my stomach, my arms were pulled out and I was pegged down to ringbolts— apparently they had specialised in this method of treatment before! A hose was forced down my throat and water turned on. I felt that I was either going to suffocate through lack of air, or drown through too much water, or burst with the pressure. It seemed that every pore of my body was oozing water; it seemed that I was being blown up like a balloon. The pain was intense. I saw bright lights. There seemed to be an immense pressure on my brain, and eventually I fainted. I was given restoratives which brought me around to consciousness again. By now I was far too weak and ill to get to my feet, so three Japanese guards supported me—I was quite a bulky man—and dragged me again to that beam from whence I had previously been

214

suspended. A Japanese officer came and said, "You look quite wet. I think it is time you were dried off. It might help you to talk more. String him up." Two Japanese guards bent suddenly and snatched my ankles from the ground, snatched so abruptly that I fell violently and banged my head on the concrete. A rope was passed around my ankles and thrown over the beam again, and while they puffed like men having a hard task, I was hoisted feet uppermost, a yard or so from the ground. Then slowly, as if they were enjoying every moment of it, the Japanese guards spread paper and a few sticks on the ground beneath me. Grinning maliciously, one struck a match and lit the paper. Gradually waves of heat came upon me. The wood ignited, and I felt the skin of my head shrivelling, wrinkling, in the heat. I heard a voice say, "He is dying. Do not let him die or I will hold you responsible. He must be made to talk." Then again a stunning thud as the rope was cast off, and I dropped head first into the burning embers. Once again I fainted.

When I regained consciousness I found that I was in a semi-basement cell lying on my back in the dank pool of water on the floor. Rats were scurrying about. At my first movement they jumped away from me, squeaking in alarm. Hours later guards came in and hoisted me to my feet, for I still could not stand. They carried me with many a prod and a curse to the iron barred window which was just level with the ground outside. Here my wrists were handcuffed to the iron bars so that my face was pressed against those bars. An officer gave me a kick and said, "You will watch all that happens now. If you turn away or close your eyes you will have a bayonet stuck into you." I watched, but there was nothing to see except this level stretch of ground—ground just about level with my nose. Soon there was a commotion at the end and a number of prisoners came into view, being propelled by guards who were treating them with excessive brutality. The group came nearer

215

and nearer, then the prisoners were forced to kneel just in front of my window. Their arms were already bound behind them. Now they were bent back like a bow, and then their wrists were tied to their ankles. Involuntarily I closed my eyes, but I was soon forced to open them as a white hot pain shot through my body. A Japanese guard had inserted a bayonet, and I could feel the blood trickling down my legs.

I looked outside. It was a mass execution. Some of the prisoners were bayoneted, others were beheaded. One poor wretch had apparently done something dreadful according to Japanese guards' standards, for he was disembowelled and left to bleed to death. This went on for several days. Prisoners were brought in front of me and executed by shooting, by bayoneting, or by beheading. The blood used to flow into my cell, and huge rats used to swarm in after it.

Night after night I was questioned by the Japanese, questioned for the information which they hoped to get out of me. But now I was in a red haze of pain, continual pain, day and night, and I hoped that they would just execute me and get it over. Then after ten days, which seemed like a hundred, I was told I was going to be shot unless I gave all the information which the Japanese wanted. The officers told me that they were sick of me, that my attitude was an insult to the Emperor. Still I declined to say anything. So I was taken back to my cell, and flung in through the door to crash, half stunned against my concrete bed. The guard turned at the door and said, "No more food for you. You won't need any after tomorrow."

As the first faint rays of light shot across the sky the next morning the door of the cell opened with a crash, and a Japanese officer and a squad of riflemen came in. I was marched out to the execution ground where I had seen so many killed. The officer pointed to the blood-saturated ground and said, "Yours will be here, too, soon. But you will have your own grave, you shall dig it." They brought a shovel, and I, prodded on by bayonets, had to dig my own shallow grave. Then I was tied to a post so that when I was shot the rope could be just cut and I would fall head first into the grave which I, myself, had dug. The officer struck a theatrical pose, as he read out the sentence which said that I was to be shot for not co-operating with the Sons of Heaven. He said, "This is your last chance. Give the information that we want or you will be sent to join your dishonoured ancestors." I made no reply—there did not seem to be anything suitable to say—so he repeated his statement. I still kept silent. At his command the squad of men raised their rifles. The officer came to me once again, and said that it really was my last chance. He emphasised it by smacking my face left and right with every word. I still made no reply, so he marked the position of my heart for the riflemen, and then for good measure he smacked my face with the flat of his sword and spat at me before turning away in disgust to rejoin his men.

Half way between me and them—but being very careful not to stand in the line of fire—he looked toward them, and gave the order to take aim. The men lifted their rifles. The barrels converged upon me. It seemed to me that the world was full of huge black holes; the black holes were the muzzles of the rifles. They seemed to grow larger and larger, ominous, and I knew that at any moment they they would spit death. Slowly the officer raised his sword, and brought it down violently with the command, "FIRE!"

The world seemed to dissolve in flame and pain, and clouds of choking smoke. I felt as if I had been kicked by giant horses with red-hot hooves. Everything spun around. The world seemed to be crazy. The last thing I saw was a red haze, blood pouring down, then blackness, a roaring blackness. Then as I sagged at my bonds—nothingness.

Later I recovered consciousness with some astonishment that the Heavenly Fields or the Other Place seemed so

217

familiar. But then everything was spoiled for me. I was resting face down in the grave. Suddenly I was prodded with a bayonet. Out of the corner of my eye I saw the Japanese officer. He said that the bullets of the execution squad had been specially prepared. "We experimented on more than two hundred prisoners," he said. They had withdrawn some of the charge, and had also removed the lead bullet and replaced it with something else, so that I should be hurt but not killed—they still wanted that information. "And we shall get it," the officer said, "we shall have to devise other methods. We will get it in the end, and the longer you hold out, the more pain you will endure."

My life had been a hard life indeed, full of rigorous training, full of self discipline, and the special training which I had had at the lamasery was the only thing which enabled me to keep going, to keep sane. It is doubtful in the extreme if anyone without that training would have been able to survive.

The bad wounds which I received at the "execution" caused double pneumonia. For the time being I was desperately ill, hovering on the brink of death, denied any medical attention at all, denied any comfort. I lay in my cell on the concrete floor without blankets, without anything, and shivered and tossed, and hoped to die.

Slowly I recovered somewhat, and for some time I had been conscious of the drone of aircraft engines, unfamiliar engines they appeared to be, too. Not the Japanese ones which I had come to know so well, and I wondered what was really happening. The prison was at a village near Hiroshima, and I imagined that the Japanese victors—the Japanese were winning everywhere—were flying back the captured aircraft.

One day when I was still very ill indeed there was a sound of aircraft engines again. Suddenly the ground shook and there was a thudding, throbbing roar. Clouds of dust fell out of the sky, and there was a stale, musty odour.

218

The air seemed to be electric, tense. For a moment nothing seemed to move. Then the guards ran in terror, screaming in fright, calling upon the Emperor to protect them from they knew not what. It was the atom bombing of Hiroshima of 6th August 1945. For some time I lay wondering what to do. Then it seemed obvious that the Japanese were far too busy to think about me, so I got shakily to my feet and tried the door. It was unlocked. I was so seriously ill that it was considered impossible for me to escape. Besides, normally there were guards about, but those guards had disappeared. There was panic everywhere. The Japanese thought that their Sun God had deserted them, and they were milling around like a colony of disturbed ants, milling around in the last extremity of panic. Rifles had been discarded, bits of uniform, food—everything. In the direction of their air raid shelters there were confused shouts and screams as they all tried to get in at the same time.

I was weak. I was almost too weak to stand. I bent to pick up a Japanese tunic and cap, and I almost fell over as giddiness overtook me. I dropped to my hands and knees, and struggled into the tunic and put the cap on. Just near there was a pair of heavy sandals. I put on these, too, because I was bare footed. Then slowly I crawled into the bushes and continued to crawl, painfully. There were many thuds and thumps, and all the anti-aircraft guns were firing. The sky was red with vast banners of black and yellow smoke. It seemed that the whole world was breaking up and I wondered at the time why I was making such an effort to get away when obviously this was the end of everything.

Throughout the night I made my slow, torturous way to the seashore, which, as I well knew, was a very few miles from the prison. I was indeed sick. The breath rasped in my throat, and my body shook and quivered. It took every bit of self control that I could muster to force myself along. At last in the dawn light I reached the shore, reached a creek. Warily, half dead with fatigue and illness, I peered out of the bushes and saw before me a small fishing boat rocking at its moorings. It was deserted. Apparently the owner had panicked and rushed off inshore. Stealthily I made my way down to it and managed painfully to pull myself upright to look over the gunwale. The boat was empty. I managed to put one foot on the rope mooring the boat, and with immense effort I levered myself up. Then my strength gave out and I toppled head first to the bottom of the boat among the bilge water and a few pieces of stale fish which apparently had been kept for bait. It took me a long time to gather enough strength to cut the mooring rope with a knife which I found. Then I slumped back into the bottom again as the vessel drifted out of the creek on the ebb tide. I made my way to the stern and crouched there utterly exhausted. Hours later I managed to hoist the ragged sail as the wind appeared favourable. The effort was too much for me and I sank back into the bottom of the boat in a dead faint.

Behind me on the mainland of Japan the decisive step had been taken. The atom bomb had been dropped and had knocked the fight out of the Japanese. The war had ended, and I knew it not. The war had ended for me, too, or so I thought, for here I was adrift upon the Sea of Japan with no food except the bits of rotten fish in the bottom, and with no water. I stood and clung to the mast for support, bracing my arms around it, putting my chin against it, holding myself up as best I could. As I turned my head toward the stern I could see the coast of Japan receding. A faint haze enveloped it. I turned toward the bows. Ahead there was nothing.

I thought of all that I had gone through. I thought of the Prophecy. As if from afar I seemed to hear the voice of my Guide, the Lama Mingyar Dondup, "You have done well, my Lobsang. You have done well. Be not disheartened, for this is not the end." Over the bows a ray of sunshine lit up the day for a moment, and the wind freshened, and the little ripplets of bow waves sprang away from the boat and made a pleasant hissing. And I? I was headed—where? all I knew was that for the moment I was free, free from torture, free from imprisonment, free from the living hell of camp life. Perhaps I was even free to die. But no, although I longed for the peace of death, for the relief that it would give me from my suffering, I knew that I could not die yet, for my Fate said that I would have to die in the land of the red man, America. And here I was afloat, alone, starving, in an open boat on the Sea of Japan. Waves of pain engulfed me. I felt once again I was being tortured. The breath rasped in my throat, and my eyes grew dim. I thought that possibly at that moment the Japanese had discovered my escape and were sending a fast boat in pursuit. The thought was too much for me. My grip of the mast slipped. I sagged, sank, and toppled, and once again I knew blackness, the blackness of oblivion. The boat sailed on into the unknown.

"KINDNESS TO PUBLISHERS" DEPARTMENT

Throughout the years since "The Third Eye" first appeared I have had a tremendous amount of mail, and up to the present I have always answered that mail. Now I have to say that I am no longer able to reply to any mail at all unless adequate return postage is enclosed. So please do NOT send letters to my Publisher for forwarding to me because I have asked my Publisher not to forward any letters.

People forget that they pay for a BOOK, and NOT a lifetime of free post-paid advisory service. Publishers are PUBLISHERS—not a letter forwarding service.

I have had letters from all over the world, even from well behind the Iron Curtain, but not one in several thousand people encloses return postage, and the cost is so much that I can no longer undertake replies.

People ask such peculiar things, too. Here are just some:

There was a very desperate letter from Australia which reached me when I was in Ireland. The matter was (apparently) truly urgent, so at my own expense I sent a cable to Australia, and I did not even receive a note of thanks.

A certain gentleman in the U.S.A. wrote me a letter DEMANDING that I should immediately write a thesis for him and send it by return airmail. He wanted to use it as his thesis to obtain a Doctorate in Oriental Philosophy. Of course he did not enclose any postage; it was merely a somewhat threatening demand!

An Englishman wrote me a very, very haughty letter in the third person, demanding my credentials. And only if they were completely satisfactory to this person would he consider placing himself under my tuition, provided that there would be no charge for it. In other words, I was supposed to be honoured. (I do not think he would like my reply!)

Another one wrote to me and said that if I "and my chums" would come from Tibet and cluster around his bed in the astral at night then he would be able to feel more happy about astral travelling.

Other people write to me and ask me everything from high esoteric things (which I can answer if I want to) to how to keep hens and one's husband! People also consider that they should write to me just whenever they think they should, and then they get offensive if I do not reply by return airmail.

I will ask you NOT to bother my Publishers, in fact I have asked them not to send on any letters to me because they are in business as Publishers. For those who really do need an answer (although I do not invite letters) I have an accommodation address. It is:

Dr T. Lobsang Rampa,
BM/TLR,
London W.C.1., England.

I do not guarantee any reply, and if you use this address you will have to provide very adequate postage because the letters will be forwarded to me and I shall have to pay, so I shall not be in a sweet enough mood to reply unless you have made my expense your expense. For example, it will cost me a dollar at least by the time forwarding charges are paid.

T. Lobsang Rampa

T. LOBSANG RAMPA

is the author of ten extraordinary books, each one immensely readable and thought provoking.

They are:

☐ **LIVING WITH THE LAMA:** More details of Lobsang Rampa's extraordinary existence—this time from a different angle! 30p
☐ **THE THIRD EYE:** A great bestseller wherever it was published. Well over 150,000 copies have been sold in the Corgi edition alone.
  30p
☐ **DOCTOR FROM LHASA:** In which Lobsang Rampa proved that mortal man can discipline his mind and body to survive starvation and torture. 30p
☐ **THE RAMPA STORY:** Revealing other aspects of the author's strange life and the mystic powers with which he is endowed. 30p
☐ **THE CAVE OF THE ANCIENTS:** Lobsang Rampa's story of his experiences at the Lamaseries of Tibet. 30p
☐ **YOU—FOR EVER:** A special course of instruction in psychic development and metaphysics. 30p
☐ **WISDOM OF THE ANCIENTS:** A book of Knowledge, with special sections on breathing exercises and diet. 30p
☐ **THE SAFFRON ROBE:** The personal story of Lobsang Rampa's boyhood at the great Lamasery of Potala. 30p
☐ **CHAPTERS OF LIFE:** Predictions and comments on the events taking place in the astral world. 30p
☐ **BEYOND THE TENTH:** Lobsang Rampa explores the spiritual potential inherent in every human being. 30p

All these books are available at your bookshop or newsagent ; or can be ordered direct from the publisher. Just tick the titles you want and fill in the form below.

CORGI BOOKS, Cash Sales Department, J. Barnicoat (Falmouth) Ltd., P.O. Box 11, Falmouth, Cornwall.

Please send cheque or postal order. No currency, and allow 5p per book to cover the cost of postage and packing in U.K. and overseas.

NAME..

ADDRESS ....

....

Rampa's Tranquilliser Touch-Stones

You are interested in the Higher Sciences or you would not be reading this book. Have you considered how your tranquillity can be nourished by a Rampa-Touch-Stone? On page 123 in *Wisdom of the Ancients* you can read about these Touch-Stones. They are available with simple instructions

AN INSTRUCTION RECORD ON MEDITATION

A large number of people wrote to Lobsang Rampa demanding a record about Meditation, so at last he has made the only special, fully authentic recording by him. Tells you how to meditate, shows you how easy it is, places peace, harmony and inner contentment within YOUR reach. Rampa-Touch-Stones Ltd. can supply this 12" record AND THE TRANQUILLISER TOUCH STONE ANYWHERE at the prices below AIRMAIL FREE.

Price List	Record	Tranquilliser Touch-Stones	
Australia	4	4.20	dollars
Austria	110	120	schillings
Belgium	220	230	francs
Canada	5.50	5.50	dollars
Denmark	30	33.5	kroner
France	20	24	francs
Great Britain	165	185	pence
Germany	17	18	deutsche marks
Holland	15	17	guilders
Italy	2500	2900	lires
New Zeland	4	4.20	dollars
Norway	30	32	kroner
S. Africa	3.5	3.8	rand
Sweden	20	25	kroner
U.S.A.	5	5	dollars

All other places £2 or $5 EACH ITEM

Rampa-Touch-Stones Ltd.
33 Ashby Road, Loughborough, Leicestershire, England.